Dark Shadows

D1713396

TV Milestones

Series Editors
Barry Keith Grant
Brock University

Jeannette Sloniowski
Brock University

TV Milestones is part of the Contemporary Approaches to Film and Television Series

A complete listing of the books in this series can be found online at wsupress.wayne.edu

General Editor
Barry Keith Grant
Brock University

Advisory Editors
Robert J. Burgoyne
University of St. Andrews

Tom Gunning
University of Chicago

Caren J. Deming
University of Arizona

Thomas Leitch
University of Delaware

Patricia B. Erens
School of the Art Institute of Chicago

Anna McCarthy
New York University

Peter X. Feng
University of Delaware

Walter Metz
Southern Illinois University

Lucy Fischer
University of Pittsburgh

Lisa Parks
University of California–
Santa Barbara

Frances Gateward
Ursinus College

ᴅARK SHADOWS

Harry M. Benshoff

TV MILESTONES SERIES

Wayne State University Press Detroit

© 2011 by Wayne State University Press,
Detroit, Michigan 48201. All rights reserved.

15 14 13 12 11   5 4 3 2 1

Library of Congress Cataloging-in-Publication Data

Benshoff, Harry M.
Dark shadows / Harry M. Benshoff.
p. cm. — (TV milestones)
Includes bibliographical references and index.
ISBN 978-0-8143-3439-3 (pbk. : alk. paper)
1. Dark shadows (Television program : 1966–1971) I. Title.
PN1992.77.D343B48 2011
791.45′72—dc22
2010037704

CONTENTS

ACKNOWLEDGMENTS

Many people contributed to this project, first and foremost being the *Dark Shadows* fans who over the course of twenty years have shared their stories, fanzines, videos, and personal recollections with me. I would also like to thank the original cast and crew of *Dark Shadows,* many of whom have also shared their stories about the series via their own memoirs, convention appearances, and video interviews produced by and for MPI Video. I also wish to thank more scholarly fans and colleagues such as Chuck Leayman, Jeff Steinbrink, Donna Cunningham, Lynn Spigel, Marsha Kinder, Leo Braudy, Drew Casper, David J. Skal, Mark Jancovich, Rick Worland, Kevin Heffernan, Travis Sutton, Derek Johnson, and Sean Griffin for their insights into gothic horror and/or serial narrative. In addition I am grateful to the administrators at the University of North Texas, who granted me a faculty development leave to work on this project during the spring of 2008.

   At Wayne State University Press, I would like to thank my commissioning editor Annie Martin, TV Milestones series co-editors Barry Keith Grant and Jeannette Sloniowski, and my outside readers for their support and helpful suggestions about

vii

the manuscript. My production team at Wayne State University Press, including Maya Rhodes, Carissa Vardanian, and Kristin Harpster Lawrence, has also been top-notch, and I thank them for their efforts.

A Cult Television Show

From June 1966 until April 1971, ABC-TV aired a daily thirty-minute soap opera titled *Dark Shadows*. The serial was unique in its subject matter, for *Dark Shadows* showcased a panoply of outright fantastic events enacted by supernatural characters such as vampires, werewolves, warlocks, and witches. Nonetheless, even within this eerie netherworld, many common soap opera narratives (alcoholism, jealousy, tangled love triangles) were also pressed into service. And like many other soap operas then and now, the show was clearly a family romance first and foremost: *Dark Shadows* tells the story of the extended Collins family of Collinsport, Maine, as it endures various supernatural tribulations throughout several centuries. Most of the show's multiple story lines were adapted (or cribbed outright) from famous gothic literary sources, including *Dracula*, *Frankenstein*, *The Turn of the Screw*, *The Lottery*, *The Picture of Dorian Gray*, *The Cthulhu Mythos*, *Dr. Jekyll and Mr. Hyde*, *Rebecca*, *Jane Eyre*, and *Wuthering Heights*. Science fiction tropes such as time travel and parallel universes were also pressed into service, and even popular horror films of the late 1960s like *Rosemary's Baby* (1968) were incorporated into *Dark Shadows* story lines. From its conception and execution then,

Dark Shadows was a unique generic hybrid, a television show that has often been touted as the world's first gothic soap opera.

Dark Shadows also differed from other soap operas of its day in terms of its reception, for the show was pitched to (and enjoyed by) children, teenagers, and young adults of both sexes as well as housewives, the thought-to-be-usual soap opera audience. Because *Dark Shadows* aired in the late afternoon, young people of the era often ran home from school or skipped college classes to watch it. Ostensibly these viewers were less interested in the show's traditional soap opera moorings and were instead attracted to the show's fantastic nature, an appeal that mirrored the era's fascination with the occult, alternative religions, and "monster culture" in general. Recognizing this, the show's producers capitalized on that appeal by heavily marketing *Dark Shadows* to its youthful audience with hit records, comic books, games, novels, and two feature films, *House of Dark Shadows* (1970) and *Night of Dark Shadows* (1971). Following its network demise in the early 1970s, *Dark Shadows* was subsequently syndicated in the United States and sold abroad in Spanish-language versions. Yet like the vampire Barnabas Collins, the show's most iconic figure, *Dark Shadows* would not stay dead and buried.

Individual fan clubs formed during the show's initial run, and they have waxed and waned in strength throughout the following decades. The first *Dark Shadows* fan convention was held in 1977, and weekend-long gatherings of fans and original cast members became annual events in the 1980s, drawing participants from all over North America. The show's fans were instrumental in bringing *Dark Shadows* reruns to public television in the 1980s, and when the cable television boom of the 1990s occurred, the Sci-Fi channel aired the show in daily strip syndication. Ongoing *Dark Shadows* fandoms were also instrumental in producer Dan Curtis's decision to remake the series as a prime-time weekly television serial that aired on NBC-TV during the spring of 1991, as well as a more recent (and aborted) adaptation for the WB network in 2004. There was even some talk of a *Dark Shadows* Broadway musical to be cowritten by Rupert Holmes, Tony-winning songsmith of *The Mystery of Edwin Drood* (1988), author of the comedic mystery *Where the Truth Lies,* and creator of the cult television hit *Remember WENN* (AMC, 1996–98). In 2008, *Dark Shadows* fans began to hear rumors of a new feature film version said to be produced by (and possibly starring) Johnny Depp and directed by Tim Burton. *Dark Shadows* is also the only American soap opera available to view and study in its entirety: MPI Video has released every episode from the show's five-year run on both home video and DVD, including one lost episode that had to be reconstructed from still photographs.

While supernatural or fantastic events on daytime television have become fairly commonplace in recent decades (a possession story line on *Days of Our Lives* [CBS, 1965–], vampires on *Port Charles* [ABC, 1997–2003], the entire concept behind *Passions* [NBC, 1999–2008]), *Dark Shadows* was first to introduce supernatural elements into the otherwise domestic milieu of the daytime soap opera. In doing so, *Dark Shadows* secured its place in television history as well as its status as a cult media text. The multifarious factors of production and reception that delineate or help create a cult media text may appear somewhat slippery, but the eight-point rubric devised by Ernest Mathijs and Xavier Mendik as a litmus test for cult movies also serves to describe *Dark Shadows* as a cult television show. *Dark Shadows* is (1) clearly an *innovative* text, bringing something new and different to the daytime serial. In so doing, the show (2) blurs and pushes at the borders of varying *fantastic genres* and creates (3) a wide array of *intertextual referentiality*—both within the show itself and across the history of gothic film and literature. Because of its hectic production schedule, complex style, and less-than-optimal budgets, *Dark Shadows* is often (4) considered cheesy or *bad,* a fact that only further endears it to many of its fans, as do its (5) *loose ends* and narrative aperture that allow viewers "the freedom of speculating on the story, and polishing or radicalizing the style on the [text's] behalf" (Mathijs and Mendik, *Cult Film Reader,* 3). And while it may seem odd to label a network-produced daytime serial as (6) *transgressive, Dark Shadows* was condemned during its initial run by some fundamentalist Christians for allegedly promoting witchcraft, while still other commentators denounced its eroticism and/or its albeit minimal (7) *gore*. Finally, *Dark Shadows* is a text deeply invested in (8) *nostalgia,* directly through its time travel narratives and indirectly through its ongoing fandoms.

Similarly, in "Defining Cult TV" Matt Hills notes that cult television texts are dependent on the dynamic sociocultural interactions between three distinct axes: (1) the primary text and its specific formal properties; (2) the show's secondary texts, that is, its official spin-off products, websites, fan magazines, reviews, and commentaries; and (3) the show's tertiary texts—those produced by its fans not for profit but out of devotion to the primary text. Again, it is easy to place *Dark Shadows* against this conceptual grid. As a primary text, *Dark Shadows* "constructs an immensely detailed, often fantastic, narrative world . . . which we as viewers can never fully encounter" (511). This is a world where central narrative enigmas—including close but questionably consummated heterosexual romances—are never fully resolved, where supernatural events occur within quotidian small-town New England. Such openness in narrative structure extends to the show's secondary texts—the multiple novels, movies, games, and comic books that reworked and re-presented the show's central themes in ever-changing forms. Finally, as will be explored in greater detail in subsequent chapters, almost forty years after its cancellation, *Dark Shadows* maintains an active fan base who continue to write their own stories, make videos, perform skits, and otherwise vicariously inhabit the haunted world of Collinsport, Maine, circa the late 1960s.

As per much contemporary work on television history, this monograph seeks to present an extended consideration—a "thick description"—of *Dark Shadows,* both during its initial run and as an enduring cult phenomenon. As such, it draws on various methodologies, including auteur and genre considerations, formal analysis, queer theories of the gothic, as well as historiography and reception theory. Toward that end, this work first explores the production contexts that gave rise to the show and then examines in some detail the particular formal ways that the show operates, and specifically how it fosters a sort of metatextual appreciation based on the aggregation of performer(s), character(s), and narrative(s). The marketing and circulation of *Dark Shadows* via its secondary texts (related books, records, reviews, commentaries, games, etc., licensed under the *Dark Shadows* brand name) further extends this aggregate, metatextual appeal, and an examination of some of those ancillary texts allows for a closer understanding of the primary text's central appeals. Finally, an examination of the show's legacy and ongoing fandoms suggests multiple things about the contemporary popularity of transmedia texts such as *Twilight* and *Harry Potter*—chiefly the importance of serialization to the creation of lucrative gothic/fantasy franchises—once again underscoring the significance of *Dark Shadows* to the history of American television and media culture-at-large.

Production History

As Elana Levine has noted in her study of *General Hospital,* the "production environment and its complicated tension of efficiency and creativity, hands-on labor and removed, hierarchical control demonstrate that struggles in soap opera production occur along cultural as well as economic lines, between duties and agendas distinguished and hierarchized by gender and institutional positioning, as well as the larger-scale constraints of ownership structure, production history, and industrial trends" ("Toward a Paradigm," 140). That said, *Dark Shadows* is nonetheless often considered to be the brainchild of television producer-director-writer Dan Curtis, who should by most accounts be considered the creative engine behind the series. As executive producer, Curtis maintained strong control over the show throughout its run, overseeing much of its day-to-day production. He occasionally directed individual episodes (as well as the two *Dark Shadows* feature films), and he had considerable input into the serial's developing story line. As Sam Hall, one of the show's best-known (and long-lasting) writers, later put it, none of the writers "had authority over the others [because] Dan Curtis was the head writer" (quoted in Scott, *Companion,* 40).

Before *Dark Shadows*, Curtis was best known for producing *CBS Golf Classics;* however, the phenomenal success of *Dark Shadows* eventually helped him develop a line of similar film and television products, including *The Night Stalker* (1972), *Trilogy of Terror* (1975), and *Burnt Offerings* (1976). In addition to adapting famous gothic novels into *Dark Shadows* story lines, Curtis also produced and/or directed multiple television movies derived from the same sources, including *The Strange Case of Dr. Jekyll and Mr. Hyde* (1968), *Dracula* (1973), and *The Turn of the Screw* (1974) (Thompson, *Television Horrors*). In fact, at least one latter-day critic refers to him as a "gothic television auteur" (Wheatley, *Gothic Television,* 13). Switching from horror to history in the 1980s, Curtis was highly acclaimed as the producer and director of the epic miniseries *Winds of War* (1983) and *War and Remembrance* (1988). Until his death in 2006, Curtis remained active in television production as well as *Dark Shadows* fandom, giving interviews about the show and helping market the project to new generations of viewers.

Dan Curtis developed *Dark Shadows* specifically for ABC, which in the mid-1960s was still considered the "third network," not only historically, but also in terms of quality productions and ratings shares. According to some television historians, this is one of the reasons ABC took more chances with its programming than did either NBC or CBS. ABC development executive Harve Bennett referred to this strategy as "wild-ass programming" (quoted in Wheatley, *Gothic Television,* 128). ABC wanted to attract viewers uninterested in the other networks' programming, to reach out to possible new viewers. In the 1960s this included the burgeoning teenage population and countercultural viewers bored with domestic sitcoms and westerns. ABC shows like *American Bandstand* (1957–97) and *Shindig!* (1964–66) featured popular youth-oriented music of the day, while many other ABC shows featured more fantastic situations. Even before *Dark Shadows* took to the air, ABC had had small hits with horror/science fiction anthology shows like

Most episodes ended with a shot of an empty set and the visual and aural reminder that "*Dark Shadows* is a Dan Curtis Production."

One Step Beyond (1959–61) and *The Outer Limits* (1963–65). One of ABC's biggest hits of the era was *Bewitched* (1964–72), a sitcom about a friendly witch who marries a mortal and is forced to adapt to suburban housewifery. (The witches and warlocks on *Dark Shadows* would be far less willing to capitulate to bourgeois norms!) Similarly, ABC's *The Addams Family* (1964–66) and CBS's *The Munsters* (1964–66) also helped to lay the groundwork for a television serial about gothic ghouls living in the modern world. Throughout the course of *Dark Shadows'* network run, ABC continued to program shows with "wild-ass" appeal, including *Voyage to the Bottom of the Sea* (1964–68), *The Invaders* (1967–68), *Time Tunnel* (1966–67), and *Land of the Giants* (1968–70). ABC's pop phenomenon *Batman* (1966–68) also aired during these years and often became a point of comparison with *Dark Shadows,* especially regarding each show's deployment of camp aesthetics (discussed more fully below).

Daytime television soap operas were still in their adolescence when *Dark Shadows* was created, having transitioned from radio formats during the mid-1950s. According to television historian Robert C. Allen, the "latter half of the 1960s was a key period in the history of U.S. daytime soap operas. By 1965 both the popularity and profitability of the television soap opera had been amply demonstrated. Soaps proved unrivaled in attracting female viewers aged between eighteen and forty-nine—the demographic group responsible for making most of the non-durable good purchasing decisions in U.S. Production costs were a fraction of those for primetime drama, and once a new soap 'found' its audience, broadcasters and advertisers knew that those viewers would be among television's most loyal" ("Soap Opera").

While still the third network, ABC premiered what would later become its daytime juggernaut *General Hospital* in 1963. It was experimenting with several other "youthful" daytime projects when *Dark Shadows* was pitched and approved for production, replacing a teen serial drama called *Never Too Young* (1965–66) on the daily schedule. Signaling its hoped-for appeal to both housewives as well as younger viewers, *Dark Shadows* was initially scheduled immediately after another soap opera, *The Nurses* (1965–67), and was followed by *Where the Action Is* (1965–74), a music show aimed at teenagers.

Although many other daytime serials of the era were owned by actual soap companies like Proctor and Gamble, *Dark Shadows* would not have a single sponsor but instead accepted ads for any number of products. Sponsors during the show's first few years included Lux hand soaps, Dream Whip food spread, Gaines dog food, Clairol hair conditioner, Woolite washing detergent, and Armor Star canned meat products. Although ABC may have been trying to target younger viewers with the show itself, a quick review of these thirty-second spots (some of which are included as bonus features on some *Dark Shadows* DVD releases) suggests that its advertisers were far more interested in targeting housewives. Almost all of them center on young white adult female protagonists as they discover new products designed to make their domestic lives easier. The style of the spots—brightly lit Madison Avenue mod—creates a curious contrast to *Dark Shadows*' gloomy diegetic spaces, arguably throwing both fictive worlds into sharper relief. Perhaps surprisingly, some of the commercials indirectly acknowledge the drudgery and/or stress of being a housewife in the mid-1960s. Ads for headache remedies like Anacin and something called Cope (a drug admixture of pain reliever and relaxant) subtly suggest that being a middle-class housewife was itself something of a toxic state. And as many viewers' responses to the show did attest, many housewives watched *Dark Shadows* precisely for its romantic escapism from the boredom of everyday life.

11

Allegedly, *Dark Shadows* was inspired by a dream Dan Curtis had about a young woman with long dark hair taking a train ride to an isolated town and then approaching a huge, forbidding mansion. Those images would indeed become the first visuals of the first episode of *Dark Shadows,* as neophyte governess Victoria Winters arrives at the Great House of Collinwood. (One can immediately note the similarity of this premise to the beginning of Charlotte Brontë's famous gothic novel *Jane Eyre,* among many others.) Curtis had considered various titles for his gothic-flavored soap opera, including *Castle of Darkness, The House on Widow's Hill, Terror at Collinwood,* and *Shadows on the Wall,* before the now-famous title was accidentally stumbled upon: in describing the lighting effect he wanted, Curtis told a technician to "go out to a museum and film some *dark shadows*" (Scott, *Companion,* 44; emphasis added). Curtis's colleague Art Wallace was brought in to create a story bible, and Wallace wrote many of the first episodes himself. In later years, Gordon Russell, Sam Hall, Ron Sproat, and Violet Welles would become the show's most prolific writers, while Lela Swift, John Sedwick, and Henry Kaplan headed its team of directors. Line producer Robert Costello worked closely with Dan Curtis and oversaw daily production, while Robert Cobert wrote the show's incidental music and its iconic main title theme, which was performed by a haunting combination of "alto flute, a double bass, vibes, a harp, and a theremin" (Scott and Pierson, *Almanac*, 148).

The *Dark Shadows* production team settled into a small Manhattan studio, and the daily grind began. The cast was anchored by aging Hollywood star Joan Bennett as reclusive matriarch Elizabeth Collins Stoddard, while younger actors (many of whom had very little experience) were hired from local summer stock stages to round out the cast. The show had a frantic production schedule, with 8:00 a.m. calls and morning read-throughs and blocking followed by makeup and costuming for the late afternoon taping. The show was shot live on tape with a standard (for that time) three video camera setup, usually one episode per day. Shows were often taped one to two weeks ahead of their airdates, although this was flexible, and occasional episodes were shot out of order as scripts and story lines underwent last-minute alterations. Music and sound effect cues, kept on large discs and later tapes, were played in the studio and recorded live along with the actors' performances. Similarly, the commercials were "rolled into" the show in real time. Wide-angle lenses were used to help expand the cramped studio sets, although the taller actors still had to duck their heads to clear the doorway under the stairs in the "Great Hall" of Collinwood. About a year into its run, *Dark Shadows* moved from black and white to color and in the process became ABC's first color soap opera. Although its black-and-white videography had allowed the show a kind of bargain basement German expressionist aesthetic, its move to color did not destroy its creepy atmosphere. If anything, as the mid-1960s became the late 1960s, the show's oddly lit sets and psychedelic dream sequences were only enhanced by the transition to color. In this respect, *Dark Shadows* might be seen as an important historical marker in the development of "televisuality," the excessive visual style that had come to characterize television production by the mid-1980s (Caldwell, *Televisuality,* 32–72).

As these points suggest, the production of *Dark Shadows* was far more complex than that of most of its daytime contemporaries. While many other soap operas of the era still used organ music to signal drama and suggest emotional response, Robert Cobert's musical cues usually employed a full orchestra. The production (especially during its first year) also made use of exterior film footage of various characters shot on location, another technique not employed by most other soap operas of the day. And as might be obvious, *Dark Shadows* used more special effects than the average daytime serial. In addition to gruesome shock effects and man-into-wolfman transition scenes, *Dark Shadows* even imported Hollywood makeup maestro Dick Smith to create a memorable "old Barnabas" for a brief run of episodes. The production also required more sets and costumes than usual: in a "given year, the series would use approximately 100 sets compared to around 30 for an average soap opera" (Scott and Pierson, *Almanac,* 130). All those sets, designed by Sy Tomashoff and lit by Mel Handelsman, had to fit into one cramped studio and were thus regularly knocked down and reassembled as needed. And although many of the costumes worn in the present-day sequences were provided by the department store Ohrbachs, costume designer Ramse Mostoller was routinely called upon to create a plethora of elaborate period costumes and wigs for the show's historical sequences. Nonetheless, *Dark Shadows* was still relatively cheaply produced, according to some estimates costing only about ten thousand dollars per episode (Brockman, "Interview"). In comparison, an episode of ABC's prime-time show *The Green Hornet* (1966) cost over ten times as much (Santo, "*Batman,*" 73).

13

Although the show would exhibit higher production values as the series went on and became increasingly popular, to present-day audiences *Dark Shadows* can seem shockingly primitive. Tombstones fall over repeatedly, "solid" stone walls shake and quiver, smoke pots can occasionally be seen within the frame, and chroma-key special effects now often seem more laughable than frightening. Furthermore, the actors frequently "went up" on their lines or stumbled through them while staring at the offscreen teleprompter. Most of these blown lines and technical gaffes went on the air (and are preserved on the video releases) because the cameras rarely stopped shooting for such "minor" errors. Retakes and edits were considered too costly and not worth the time and effort. Not realizing that the show would someday become a cult hit and be preserved on digital media, the actors and technicians responsible for said gaffes often comforted themselves with the erroneous belief that the episode would only be aired once and never seen again.

The *Dark Shadows* production team kept up this hectic pace for almost five years. Although many of the actors and technicians could be rotated in and out of the production schedule as dictated by the scripts, some of the most popular actors remained in the studio on an almost daily basis. Many were also expected to make grueling public appearance tours, appearing in parades and at supermarket openings in order to promote the show (Scott and Pierson, *Almanac,* 193–96). When the two *Dark Shadows* feature films were made in upstate New York, shuttle buses carried actors back and forth from Manhattan so that they could work on both projects simultaneously. By the time the series slipped in the ratings far enough for its cancellation, it had nonetheless amassed a passionate following. The last episode of *Dark Shadows* aired on April 2, 1971, and the series was replaced by yet another incarnation of the long-running game show *Password.*

Chapter 2

A Necessarily Brief Synopsis

Although *Dark Shadows* reached the apex of its popularity as a soap opera when it was centered on a reluctant vampire named Barnabas Collins, at its inception the show did not feature supernatural characters at all. Instead it used its gothic atmosphere as a backdrop for more realist intrigues at Collinwood, the brooding ancestral estate of adult siblings Elizabeth and Roger Collins. Early story lines centered on Roger's possible involvement with several mysterious deaths; Roger's unruly and morbid son, David; and David's new governess Victoria Winters (who is vaguely intimated but never proven to be Elizabeth's illegitimate daughter). Rounding out the basic-but-broken nuclear family living at the Great House are Elizabeth's teenage daughter, Carolyn; groundskeeper Matthew Morgan; and housekeeper Mrs. Johnson. Also in the cast are various locals who inhabit the fishing village of Collinsport, Maine, including fisherman Joe Haskell, waitress Maggie Evans, and her father, Sam, an alcoholic painter. Much time is spent developing a rivalry between the Collins family and entrepreneur Burke Devlin, a man who was sent to prison when Roger and Sam testified falsely against him in court. However, during the show's first months on the air, ratings were poor and Dan Curtis was told by ABC to improve them or else. In retrospect, one of the reasons for the show's initial low ratings may have been its lack of a strong romance; Carolyn and her boyfriend Joe were far from passionate lovers, and various early attempts to link Burke Devlin with Victoria (or with Carolyn) were not pursued by the writers to any great degree.

Whether by desperation or design, the show became increasingly supernatural, adding first a few ghosts (including the protective spirit of ancestor Josette Collins) and then the character of Laura Murdoch Collins, Roger's estranged wife who returns to Collinwood to claim their son, David. Eventually, Laura is revealed to be a "phoenix," a creature that can be consumed by fire but is also resurrected every one hundred years. It was with this story line that the show began to hit its stride.

Most of the stylistic and narrative elements that would "click" when Barnabas Collins was added to the milieu a few months later were either already in place or developed during this story arc. Like Barnabas, Laura is a long-lost member of the Collins family who mysteriously appears and takes up residence on the estate (but not at the Great House itself). Laura poses a threat to young David Collins and other members of the extended family, as well as painter Sam Evans, who is compelled to paint portraits of Laura surrounded by flames. (The gothic literary tropes of haunted portraiture and similar doppelgänger effects would become ongoing motifs throughout the run of the show.) Just as Barnabas will have, Laura has supernatural powers that she uses to control others from a distance (as when she puts Elizabeth into a trance), and her iconic "hypnotic power" shot (sitting before her raging fireplace in the Collins cottage) presages a similar shot of Barnabas glowering out the window of the Old House, calling his minions to his side. As Barnabas will do repeatedly, Laura enters the Great House through supernatural means, appearing in sleeping characters' bedrooms to work her wiles. The effect of Laura "materializing" out of the shadows was created via a simple and soon-to-be much-employed lighting technique: studio technicians slowly increased the amplitude of a lamp positioned close to the floor and angled upright on the actor, making it appear as if Laura has magically appeared out of the shadows.

Perhaps most important to the show's future narrative development, once the Collins family begins to suspect that there is something "wrong" about Laura, a researcher who specializes in psychic/supernatural phenomena is brought in to investigate. Although Laura eventually kills this figure (Dr. Peter Guthrie), his character was the prototype for Dr. Julia Hoffman and Professor T. Eliot Stokes, two later characters who would remain on the show until its demise, investigating and explaining the supernatural occurrences at Collinwood. Still other familiar tropes of the series are introduced during Laura's story

Predating Barnabas by several months, the mysterious Laura Collins (Diana Millay) appears from the shadows to menace governess Victoria Winters (Alexandra Moltke).

line: séances are held, the crumbling Old House on the estate is explored, and graves are exhumed as the "monster" and her investigator play a cat and mouse game. The ghost of Josette Collins eventually aids the family in discovering the truth about Laura and saving David from her fiery clutches. (Not every supernatural creature at Collinwood is necessarily hostile to those living there, an important aspect of the serial's reworking of usual gothic/horror tropes.) As Laura goes up in flames at the end of her story line, ambitious fire effects—along with lighting and in-camera effects—were employed in the studio, a trend that would also be exploited over the years as episodes increasingly began to end with a cliff-hanger centered on some sort of startling supernatural effect.

To replace Laura (who also had to die within the story line because the actress playing her was pregnant), Dan Curtis decided to introduce Barnabas Collins, a 175-year-old vampire. Barnabas takes up residence at the Old House on the Collinwood estate, passing himself off to the family and locals as a distant cousin from England. His manservant Willie Loomis, previously a petty thief, watches over his coffin by night and renovates the Old House by day. Although the vampire narrative was planned as only a short story arc, Barnabas proved to be so popular that he became the show's central protagonist. Needing to soften him from monster/killer to a more complex ongoing character, the writers began to give him regrets about his monstrous status. The ghost of Sarah Collins, Barnabas's sister from long ago, returns to chide him, a narrative device that allows Barnabas to display human emotions like remorse. At this point, Barnabas becomes a gothic hero in the classical literary sense, a brooding man of mystery who attracts various love interests. First and foremost among these is local waitress Maggie Evans, whom Barnabas kidnaps and tries to make over into the persona of his long-lost lover, Josette DuPres. (This Barnabas-and-Josette "super-coupling" plays out repeatedly over the course of the show's run, as Barnabas often romances women who either *are* Josette or who *may be* her in some reincarnated or Parallel Time form.) When Maggie/Josette is hidden away from Barnabas in Wyndcliff Sanitarium, he begins to pay attention to governess Victoria Winters, who is intrigued by his old-world charm and the nostalgic tales he tells of Collinwood's history. Barnabas also comes under the scrutiny of Maggie's psychiatrist Dr. Julia Hoffman, a forty-something professional woman who first plans to destroy him but who also falls in love with him. Although Barnabas is initially quite hostile to Julia (and never reciprocates her unspoken love for him), as the series progresses they too become close allies, another sort of "super-couple" perhaps, but one dedicated to protecting the "normal" inhabitants of Collinwood rather than personal romance.

19

The reluctant vampire Barnabas Collins (Jonathan Frid) was both a frightening monster as well as a romantic leading man.

Late in 1967, the show entered its first historical flashback sequence in order to dramatize the origins of Barnabas's vampirism. Via a séance, governess Victoria Winters finds herself transported to (and trapped in) the year 1795. There, the original human Barnabas is about to wed his beloved Josette DuPres. However, Barnabas has also had a fling with Josette's beautiful blonde maid Angelique, who has other plans for the nuptial couple. Practicing witchcraft, Angelique torments the Collins family and eventually curses Barnabas with vampirism; the revelation of that causes Josette to leap to her death from Widow's Hill. Because of her uncanny status in 1795, Victoria Winters is mistaken for the witch and persecuted by various Collins family members and a fire-and-brimstone preacher named Reverend Trask. As Victoria is about to be hanged, she is magically returned to the present day (1968), and from there the story resumes its contemporary narrative.

By 1968 *Dark Shadows* was riding a wave of popularity, and the show's gothic story lines went into overdrive. Angelique shows up at modern-day Collinwood in a mod floral print dress and a close-cut black wig as Cassandra Collins, Roger's new wife. (Intriguingly, the same trope would be employed one year later on *Bewitched,* as blonde Samantha began to interact with her dark-haired cousin Serena, both played by Elizabeth Montgomery.) Cassandra's witchy ways are now overseen by the warlock Nicholas Blair. Dr. Eric Lang, who is creating a Frankenstein-like creature named Adam, is able to cure Barnabas of his vampirism for a short period of time, but Angelique's ongoing "dream curse" is designed to return him to his vampiric status once again. After Dr. Lang dies, Dr. Hoffman becomes involved in his experiments, bringing Adam to life and creating a bride for him named Eve. Nicholas Blair turns Angelique into a vampire and attempts to use Adam and Eve as possible conduits to spread evil throughout the world. Meanwhile, a werewolf prowls the grounds, and various other vampires and victims continue to bite and be bitten. All of these (and many other) story lines eventually gave way to a *Turn of the Screw*–inspired plot in which the silent ghost of Quentin Collins begins to menace Collinwood children David and Amy. New governess Maggie Evans (Like Laura, Victoria was written out of the show after the actress playing her became pregnant) tries to save the children, but (as in the Henry James novel) young David drops dead at her feet, prompting yet another historical flashback in the overall story line.

The 1897 narrative explains the origins of the tall, dark, and handsome Quentin Collins, who quickly became almost as popular with the fans as Barnabas. In this story line, Barnabas (aided and abetted by Julia Hoffman and paranormal researcher Professor Stokes) travels back in time via I-Ching wands in order to change history and bring David back to life. The vampiric Barnabas awakens in his coffin in 1897 but is soon let out and protected by the gypsies Magda and Sandor. As in his initial story line, Barnabas arrives at the Great House of Collinwood and once again passes himself off as a distant cousin from England, all the while creating vampiric mayhem in and around the estate. (In a surprise move, Barnabas is hunted down and staked on camera; however, his "dead" body is later revealed to be a supernatural doppelgänger.) The 1897 flashback sequence also replays the first season's phoenix story line, with Laura Collins showing up to claim her children. The now-human Quentin is a bachelor playboy, having bedded both Laura and Magda's sister Jenny (who as a madwoman still haunts the tower room at Collinwood). As vengeance for what he did to Jenny, Magda curses Quentin and his descendents with lycanthropy. Quentin's curse is eventually reversed when Count Petofi, an eccentric sorcerer, commissions a portrait that drains off the werewolf curse, keeping Quentin eternally young in the process. After much more mayhem and many more plot developments, Count Petofi is destroyed, and Barnabas starts his return to the future, the contemporary year 1969.

The roguish Quentin Collins (David Selby), seen here in a collectible postcard, was costumed and coiffed to suggest both the swinging 1960s as well as the Victorian era.

The show then began to follow a plotline loosely based on H. P. Lovecraft's *The Cthulhu Mythos,* a series of pulp horror stories from the 1920s that center on a group of otherworldly creatures trying to inhabit and take over Earth. Thus, somewhere in time between 1897 and 1969, Barnabas is captured and brainwashed by the Leviathans, a group of mysterious robed people who give him a strange "Naga" box that contains the life essence of their leader. Barnabas enlists the aid of local antique shop owners Megan and Philip Todd, who oversee the development of the life essence in a young man named Jeb Hawkes, who has designs on Carolyn. Although normal-looking, Jeb is supposedly truly monstrous in his actual form; however, the show never reveals this sight, as it was probably beyond the scope of its technical capacities. Meanwhile, warlock Nicholas Blair returns to assist the Leviathans, and various other people are drawn into the conspiracy even as Barnabas once again reverts to his vampiric self and begins to oppose them. A present-day Quentin (now immortal from his magical portrait) also returns to Collinwood, while other assorted vampires and werewolves plague the estate.

As these story lines petered out (most fans agree that the Leviathan story line was slow moving and somewhat uninteresting, perhaps because it never had a payoff in the form of a monstrous Jeb Hawkes), *Dark Shadows* once again shifted into a brand new narrative sequence: Parallel Time. Via a mysterious room in the East Wing of Collinwood, Barnabas enters another dimension where everyone at Collinwood looks familiar but leads very different lives. Practically, this move gave the writers yet another clean slate, and they began to spin new stories along with the tried-and-true one of vampiric Barnabas posing as a distant cousin from England. In this dimension, Quentin is acting head of the Collins household, Maggie is his wife, and Roger and Elizabeth are the poor relations. Parallel Time 1970 features a *Dr. Jekyll and Mr. Hyde* story line, as well as a story line based on *Rebecca* (with Angelique as both the dead mistress of Collinwood and her twin sister Alexis). Ironically, in Parallel Time, Barnabas's "real-world" ally Dr. Julia Hoffman is now a "Mrs. Danvers" housekeeper figure who tries to stake Barnabas. Fortunately, the "real" Julia arrives, kills her Parallel Time self, and takes her place so that she may continue to aid Barnabas in his investigations. Barnabas also finds a new love interest in Parallel Time, a young redhead named Roxanne Drew, but they are separated as Barnabas and Julia are transported to the future, the "real" year of 1995, where they find Collinwood in ruins and haunted by the malevolent ghost of Gerard Stiles.

Returning to present-day Collinwood in 1970, *Dark Shadows* began to work yet another variation on the *Turn of the Screw* story. Children David Collins and Hallie Stokes are possessed by two children from 1840 who look just like them; they also begin to see the ghosts of Gerard Stiles and Daphne Harridge. As Gerard summons an army of zombies to destroy Collinwood, Julia discovers a "staircase in time" that takes her to Collinwood in the year 1840. There she releases Barnabas from his coffin and they present themselves to the 1840 Collinses as—surprise!—distant cousins from England. The story now revolves around the disembodied head of warlock Judah Zachary, whose malevolent spirit eventually enters the body of Gerard Stiles in an attempt to avenge himself on the Collins family. The show's final narrative sequence takes place in Parallel Time 1841 and features plotlines borrowed from *Wuthering Heights* and *The Lottery*. In the show's final episode, a young woman is discovered with a strange wound on her neck, but a voice-over announcer assures the audience that it was not in fact a vampire bite but the bite of a wild animal and that for the first time in many years, "the dark shadows at Collinwood were but a memory of the distant past."

Macronarrative
Adapting the Gothic Novel and the Horror Film

As is hopefully apparent by this brief (and woefully incomplete) synopsis, *Dark Shadows* was a densely plotted and (compared to many of its contemporaries) quickly moving soap opera. Its dependence on story lines from classic gothic novels was perhaps its greatest strength as well as its biggest weakness. The show's writers did indeed keep a listing of well-known gothic texts that they would consult and adapt as needed, thus bringing classic, complex, and familiar story lines to the show. Yet, at the same time, such cribbing from other sources was severely limiting. As Jonathan Frid (who played Barnabas) later observed, the writers "went through all the stories three or four times. We started repeating ourselves, and the show burned out" (quoted in Scott, *Companion*, 172). This issue of adaptation was fairly unique to *Dark Shadows*—although other soap operas of the era undoubtedly borrowed narratives from women's romances and Hollywood melodramas, it was much more obvious that *Dark Shadows* was rewriting a fairly limited number of classic gothic texts. Furthermore, the history of *Dark Shadows* itself mirrors the twentieth-century evolution of the gothic novel into the more forthright monster-centered horror film: the show may have started out by recalling the brooding gothic romance of *Jane Eyre,* but it soon began to focus on vampires, werewolves, and Frankenstein monsters.

This chapter explores how *Dark Shadows* adapted these closed forms (novels and films) into an open-ended serial format. Although the show often employed gothic tropes and horrific motifs in accordance with their classical uses and meanings (to create a sense of frightening otherness), the adaptation of gothic horror into a soap opera format also changed some of the genre's usual ideological effects. Most specifically, by removing narrative closure, *Dark Shadows* rarely reaffirmed stability or "normality" as an ongoing or desirable state. In fact, the various counterhegemonic impulses of the gothic novel and/or the horror film are exacerbated within the format of a gothic soap opera like *Dark Shadows,* which more often celebrates rather than rebukes the perversity of its gothic characters. (Granted, the serial nature of most nongothic soap operas also undermines the static "normality" of everyday life, but in most instances the "normal" soap opera still maintains and privileges the ideologies of white heteronormative capitalism.)

The genres of gothic literature and television soap opera may be more similar than one might realize upon first consideration. As historian of the gothic genre Richard Davenport-Hines rather succinctly puts it, with its litany of "confused paternities, improbable coincidences, melodrama, sudden death, cheap ideas, [and] trivially stereotyped characters [the] television soap opera provides the twentieth century equivalent of gothic novels" (quoted in Wheatley, *Gothic Television,* 148–49). To be more specific, gothic literature is characterized by certain generic traits including (1) a mediated or otherwise self-reflexive narrative; (2) flamboyant villains who are characterized in greater detail than the otherwise stereotypical "normal" heroes and heroines; (3) physical settings—usually old or decaying buildings—that mirror the interior state of the gothic (anti)hero; and (4) supernatural events and effects designed to arouse fear or terror in the reader (MacAndrew, *Gothic Tradition,* 3–52).

Dark Shadows could and did easily adapt those tropes. The show's heavy reliance on flashbacks, flash-forwards, dream sequences, and Parallel Time zones complicates and confounds linear narrative structure(s). Similarly, the voice-over narration that opens each episode draws attention to *Dark Shadows* as a tale being told. And as should be obvious from the above synopsis, *Dark Shadows* showcased many bigger-than-life villains whose stories were always more interesting than those of the "normal" people with whom they interacted. These "villains" should perhaps be more precisely referred to as gothic (anti) heroes, for even though characters like Barnabas, Quentin, Angelique, Jeb, and Gerard do nefarious things, they are nonetheless tragic romantic figures whose evil natures are often forced upon them against their own wills. Thus, another common aspect of the soap opera's narrative format—turning villains into heroes and vice versa—made it well suited for adapting and dramatizing gothic tales whose most interesting figures are both villainous and heroic. Despite the show's budgetary shortcomings and physically limited studio spaces, *Dark Shadows* created numerous iconic spaces that were used to mirror the souls of its gothic villains. Barnabas's candlelit coffin room and noir-lit parlor in the Old House suggest his shadowy antiquity, while Quentin's study at Collinwood contains an antique Victrola that mournfully comments on his tragic romanticism. Finally, in accordance with classic gothic literature, *Dark Shadows* regularly produced shock effects and moments of terror (sometimes at the expense of logic or narrative development), some of which can still create a frisson of unease for contemporary viewers.

In her book *Gothic Television,* Helen Wheatley further expands on these narrative tropes to include "a proclivity towards the structures and images of the uncanny (repetitions, returns, déjà vu, premonitions, ghosts, doppelgangers, animated inanimate objects and severed body parts, etc.); and, perhaps most importantly, homes and families which are haunted, tortured or troubled in some way" (3). Again, those traits are central to the world of *Dark Shadows,* where portraits, mirrors, and books are often haunted or seem to have lives of their own, and crystal balls, tarot cards, and I-Ching wands are used to foreshadow narrative events. In more specific instances, at one point in the narrative the severed hand of Count Petofi becomes a magical talisman; in another sequence the disembodied head of Judah Zachary commands attention and imposes its will on others. And if gothic literature is always about a troubled home/family life in some way (recall Freud's formulation of the uncanny as something slightly askew within the "homely" or quotidian), then, Wheatley notes, gothic television is doubly uncanny. In watching it, she argues, "we are constantly reminded that this is terror/horror television which takes place, and is *viewed,* within a domestic milieu" (ibid., 7). Thus, she continues, "the uncanny can be found in the very structure of Gothic television: it is located in its repetitions and returns, in an aesthetic which combines traditionally realist, familiarizing program making and non-naturalistic, disorienting filming and editing" (ibid.). Certainly this describes the very structure and style of *Dark Shadows* as it wedded the conventional daytime televisual form of the 1960s to elaborate dream sequences and special effects–laden supernatural sequences. In her analysis of *Dark Shadows* itself, Wheatley notes the same domestic/gothic pairing within the diegetic space of Collinwood: the Great House is inhabited by the "normal" family, while the decaying Old House is inhabited by the vampire Barnabas.

In addition to the sights and sounds and themes of gothic literature, *Dark Shadows* also adapts the iconography of the classical Hollywood horror film (itself partly derived from gothic literature). Rarely does a week of episodes occur without clanking chains, howling dogs, screams in the night, and/or dark clouds passing over the face of the moon. However, while *Dark Shadows* uses the horror genre's semantic form to set an eerie, disturbing tone, the horror genre's syntactic narrative structure—and its subsequent thematic/ideological effect—had

The gothic trope of the mirror helps to suggest that Lady Kitty Soames (Kathryn Leigh Scott) in 1897 may actually be the reincarnation of Josette DuPres from 1795.

to undergo revision as it was adapted into soap opera form. Arguably the chief difference between a classical Hollywood horror film (or a gothic novel or an episode of a gothic/horror anthology show) and *Dark Shadows* is the latter's lack of narrative closure. This facet both extends and alters the usual effects of gothic horror. On the one hand, the soap opera's much-re-marked-on preference for paradigmatic character development over syntagmatic plotlines enables *Dark Shadows* to feature rich and complicated gothic characters. On the other hand, gothic tales and horror movies follow an Aristotelian narrative curve and resolve with climax and denouement, while soap operas do not. Thus as Wheatley again notes, "The open-ended soap-style narrative lends itself very well to the Gothic, as a genre of uncertainty" (ibid., 148).

In point of fact, this tension between closure and aperture is evidenced throughout the run of *Dark Shadows:* some of its story lines come to resolution while others do not. For example, at the end of each narrative sequence set in a past historical era (or in the Parallel Time universe), villains can be killed, romances can be finalized, and plots can be (somewhat) resolved. Thus in the 1897 sequence, archvillain Count Petofi and his henchman Aristede are destroyed, never to return again throughout the rest of serial's run. To some extent, *Dark Shadows* might be considered as a series of shorter interlocking serials, more along the formal lines of the Spanish-language telenovela. Its narrative complexity also presages the formal experimentation of more recent prime-time serials such as *The X-Files* (Fox, 1993–2002), *Lost* (ABC, 2004–10), and *Six Feet Under* (HBO, 2001–5) (see Mittell, "Narrative Complexity"; Newman, "Beats to Arcs"; and Sconce, "What If?"). However, although each of *Dark Shadows'* historical or Parallel Time sequences might be excerpted and enjoyed as stand-alone texts (especially now that the show exists primarily on DVD), it is the paradigmatic character relationships that exist across these various story lines which provide the narrative "glue" for ultimately holding the entire series together. Thus, it is the presence of ongoing and eternal supernatural characters such as Barnabas, Quentin, and Angelique (as well as the time-transcending romances of Barnabas and Josette, Barnabas and Julia, or Barnabas and Angelique) that comprise *Dark Shadows'* paradigmatic narrative. This is an ongoing structural effect impossible to achieve in single closed texts such as the gothic novel or the horror film.

The usual ideological effects of the horror film, perhaps most succinctly defined by Robin Wood as "normality . . . threatened by the Monster" (*Hollywood,* 78), are also suspended or altered by *Dark Shadows'* structure as a soap opera. In the classical Hollywood horror film (as opposed to more modern horror films) "normality" eventually overcomes and defeats the monster, suggesting the desirability of the status quo. Because of this, as Wood has postulated, much horror cinema before the 1970s (as well as since the rise of the slasher film in the 1980s) can and should be considered reactionary because of its climactic and violent recapitulation to white patriarchal norms. Thus the foreign aristocrat Count Dracula must be destroyed by a mixture of macho heroics and the scientific/Christian discourses of Professor Van Helsing. *Dark Shadows,* however, while still embracing the tropes of female seduction and/or rape by gothic (anti)heroes, cannot by its serial nature effect permanent closure and the reinstatement of "norms," patriarchal or otherwise. To a great extent, *Dark Shadows* constructs much of its narrative pleasure around the audience's identification with its supernatural characters, both male and female, and not their eventual recapitulation to patriarchal figures and institutions. As noted previously, *Dark Shadows* constantly blurs the line between normality and the monstrous. Monsters are "softened" into (anti)heroes, and normal people frequently acquire or are transformed via supernatural powers. Like the more recent novel and film version of *Interview with the Vampire* (1994), *Dark Shadows* is more about its gothic characters' struggles with their own desires and identities than any attempt to vanquish him or her in the name of the traditional moral order.

It has also been argued that the television soap opera—even when nongothic—is potentially more challenging to normative perspectives and dominant ideologies than its immediate progenitor, the radio soap opera. In general, radio soap operas were shorter than television soap operas, had relatively smaller casts, and were always grounded by a unifying voice-over narrator who allegedly spoke for the status quo of white patriarchal capitalism. As Robert C. Allen puts it, "The removal of narrational power from the 'top' in the television soap opera narrative and the dispersal of norms throughout the community of characters serves to 'open up' the soap opera text to the expression of a greater variety of perspectives" (*Speaking,* 171). Although Allen maintains that this shift makes "more covert the overall normative perspective represented by the text," as characters representing nonnormative values can always be dropped from the show or "attitudinally 'defused'" (ibid., 171), *Dark Shadows*' supernatural characters rarely disappear from the text altogether. Furthermore, the supposedly "normal" denizens of Collinsport are frequently bland and/or naive and relatively underdeveloped as characters in comparison to the supernatural ones. They do little to defuse or challenge the nonnormative ideologies inherent in the vampire, the witch, or the warlock. One might even argue that at Collinwood, vampires, witches, and warlocks are themselves normative.

Following Robin Wood's famous formulation of the horror film's monster as white patriarchal capitalism's repressed Other, one can then understand *Dark Shadows*' vampires, mad scientists, and transformation monsters as queer forces that disrupt heteronormative patriarchy. At Collinwood, "normality" is always already in a state of ongoing unease. Furthermore, specific narrative threads throughout the run of the show actively critique patriarchal structures such as the nuclear family and Christianity. For example, there is never much patriarchal stability at Collinwood; matriarch Elizabeth controls the purse strings, and most of the actual fathers who live there (like Roger) are rather weak and/or ineffectual. (Joshua Collins, from the 1795 sequence, is one of the few strong fathers on the show—but he is written and acted as overbearing and oppressive; he also succumbs to the witch Angelique's spells at various points.) There are traditionally naive gothic heroines within the text, but there are also strong professional women who more forcefully drive (and even write) the narrative instead of being acted upon by it. Perhaps most remarkably, the one unregenerate and truly unsympathetic villain on the show is the willfully hypocritical Reverend Trask, a character who in 1795 persecutes innocent women and whose descendant in 1897 murders his own wife. Furthermore, many of the sexist codes of classical Hollywood representation are inverted within the text: men become spectacularized objects of the gaze far more frequently than do women. And, as many *Dark Shadows* fans and creators have discerned, there is also the occasional hint of the homoerotic lurking in the shadows of Collinwood, with several male-male master/servant couples (Jason and Willie, Barnabas and Willie, Count Petofi and Aristede) ripe for homoerotic appropriation.

Examining marriage—arguably the prime institution both defining and reinforcing heteronormative patriarchy—on *Dark Shadows* further supports the thesis that Collinwood is best understood as a place of counterhegemonic impulses. It is a given that many marriages on even "normal" soap operas do often "go wrong," as serial story lines demand conflict and not domestic

The show's most unredeemable villain, the hypocritical Christian minister Reverend Trask (Jerry Lacy), is seen here in a fairly typical extreme close-up shot.

bliss; however, they are nonetheless celebrated as elaborate and central rituals important to the plot and to the diegetic community. On *Dark Shadows*, however, weddings are almost completely absent. Most occur offscreen or are called off at the last minute due to supernatural events. (It is also doubtful that the show's budget could have been increased to allow for a cast of more than five or six characters per episode, a seeming requirement of a large and happy soap opera wedding.) More regularly, weddings on *Dark Shadows* are figured as some sort of gothic perversion of the heteronormative ceremony, as when warlock Nicholas Blair turns his wedding to Maggie Evans into a Black Mass. Similarly, in the 1970 Leviathan sequence, Carolyn marries Jeb Stuart, although the audience knows that he is really a hideous alien creature in human guise. The heteronormative results of marriage—children—are also somewhat perverted on the show. Far from being the epitome of innocence and heterosexual grace, David Collins is morbid and murderous, Sarah Collins is a ghost, and Quentin's children either die or carry on his curse of lycanthropy. Child actor David Henesy, who played David as well as Jamison Collins, even got to play an archvillain for a spate of episodes when his body was possessed by the spirit of Count Petofi in the 1897 sequence.

Perhaps more generally, serialization produces a distinctly different kind of subject position for the spectator than either a gothic novel or a classical Hollywood horror film. As Tania Modleski put it in her groundbreaking study of the form, "Soap operas continually insist on the insignificance of the individual life" (*Loving,* 91), and in so doing, even "normal" soap operas encourage the spectator to embrace multiple characters and subject positions. Aside from its large cast of characters, this is schematized in *Dark Shadows* in many other ways. For example, "normal" characters undergo identity transformations when they are bitten by a vampire or are placed under a magical spell or curse. In one remarkable narrative thread from the 1897 episodes, Count Petofi avenges himself upon the denizens of Collinwood by means of a transformational kiss that causes each individual subject to reveal his or her "true" hidden self. Thus the master of Collinwood becomes its butler, and Charity Trask, the upright and uptight daughter of the hypocritical minister, finds herself possessed by the spirit of Pansy Faye, a freewheeling songstress and hard-drinking burlesque performer. With such transformations occurring on a regular basis, *Dark Shadows* seems to dramatize a poststructuralist model of human subjectivity, one that stresses a fluid, performative notion of identity rather than some form of static essentialist individuality. The way the show was cast, with many actors playing more than one role, also contributes to this effect.

There are several other ways that *Dark Shadows*' serial form counters patriarchal assumptions. One is by its very status as a "low" or disreputable form of popular culture. Like its antecedents the gothic novel, the horror film, and the (nongothic) soap opera, *Dark Shadows* is focused on sensation over intellect, a facet of its appeal that aligns it with the traditionally feminine rather than the masculine. As Linda Williams might put it, all of these textual forms are "body genres" (analogous to pornography and physical comedy), in that they create pleasure primarily via the spectators' bodily response (weeping, laughing, screaming) rather than by rational argument or intellectual engagement. Theorist D. A. Miller takes this argument even further when he applies it to the process of decoding the "sensation" novel. He suggests that the text of terror actively "feminizes" its reader, even when the reader being addressed within the text is supposedly male. According to Miller, if we accept that "nervousness remains a signifier of femininity" and that "the [sensation] novel makes nervousness a metonymy for reading," then the reader is situated by the text to "identify with nerve-racked figures" and to experience the "thrill" of the traditionally feminine (*Novel*, 151).

However, although *Dark Shadows* may create queer gender-bending pleasures by encouraging multiple identifications with supernatural figures and victims of both sexes, it is also dependent on the patriarchal stereotype of the hysterical young woman who is always ready to scream, faint, or fly away into flights of romantic fancy. It might be argued that *Dark Shadows,* like the gothic novel or the horror film in general, places some of its female characters "back where they belong," in the world of the traditionally feminine. The show's generic ingenue figures (including Victoria, Carolyn, and Maggie) do have a limited range of narrative functions, especially when compared to matriarch Elizabeth Collins Stoddard, witch Angelique, or vampire hunter/mad scientist Dr. Julia Hoffman. And as will be discussed in subsequent chapters, some women in the *Dark Shadows* audience could, did, and do respond to the pleasures of identifying with the show's passive female characters as the victims of gothic rape or seduction. Other viewers read these characters as dangerously naive, while still other female characters on the show (such as ditsy Millicent or the luckless and often comatose Sabrina) can almost be read as parodies of the gothic ingenue. Ultimately, the ideological effects of *Dark Shadows* depend not only on how the show adapted gothic horror narratives to soap opera form but also on its daily episodic structure, as well as the reading perspectives brought to the text by its individual readers.

Chapter 4

Micronarrative
Television Melodrama and Episodic Structure

As theorists Jane Feuer and David Thorburn have previously argued, much televisual form is inherently melodramatic, but in ways often quite distinct from the melodrama of stage or screen. Classical and postclassical Hollywood melodramas (like those of Nicholas Ray or Douglas Sirk) are often associated with a formally excessive mise-en-scène; however, many televisual narratives of the 1960s and 1970s could not supply such formal excess due to budgetary restrictions and the small size of the TV screen. That era's television melodramas created excess in other ways—through the use of close-ups, match cuts, zoom shots, a heightened (some might say nonnaturalistic) performance style, as well as consistent musical underscoring and use of musical "stingers" to exacerbate conflict. Emphasizing the "melo" as well as the drama, certain characters on *Dark Shadows* even have their own leitmotifs: composer Robert Cobert wrote melancholy airs specifically associated with Maggie, Quentin, and Angelique that were used repeatedly on the show to signify their overweening gothic romanticism. As Wheatley again notes of the show, "Melodrama can be seen as the generic link between *Dark Shadows*' two hybrid genres, the soap opera and the Gothic drama" (*Gothic Television,* 152). *Dark Shadows* employs all the usual codes of television melodrama as outlined by Feuer and Thorburn, but its nascent televisuality also allowed for more cinematic visuals effects, as discussed below.

In its daily format, *Dark Shadows* maintained a fairly rigid narrative structure. Each episode begins with a "teaser" sequence in which an offscreen narrator speaks over several exterior establishing shots of Collinwood. This narration is accompanied by music that connotes a sense of unease. For the first few years, actress Alexandra Moltke as governess Victoria Winters always spoke this introduction ("My name is Victoria Winters . . ."); when she left the show, a variety of other actors on the show took over the job. This voice-over functions very differently from the extradiegetic narrator of the radio soap opera however, who tended to impose ideological coherence on the text, as well as serve as spokesman for the products being sold. Victoria's voice-over does not hawk products or overtly moralize about characters and events (even as it does situate Victoria as a normative voice within the narrative) but sets the gothic mood, as she often describes ongoing events in sinister or foreboding terms. The "purple prose" of the voice-over also deliberately invokes a gothic literary tradition and immediately anchors the show within its generic moorings.

As the voice-over ends, the first scene of each episode begins with a dissolve from an exterior establishing shot (actually a still photographic image of an exterior scene) to a studio interior set. In many cases, especially as the show moved beyond its first year, the teaser segment was a repeat and/or extension of the preceding episode's climactic moments; as such, the teaser invariably ends on a dramatic climax accompanied by a musical stinger. After a fade to black, a brief title sequence consisting of three shots of crashing waves identifies the show and further establishes a gothic atmosphere. The title "Dark Shadows" appears over the shots of the waves, and remains on-screen over a final matching dissolve from crashing waves to an exterior shot of Collinwood at night. When the show moved to color in the summer of 1967, an additional shot of crashing waves was inserted, and the "Dark Shadows" title—still in a gothic-looking font—"rolled" into place, suggesting the movement of the ocean. In fact, the title sequence is designed to suggest maximum impact and conflict: the first shot shows waves moving from left to right, the second reverses that screen direction, while the third shows the waves headed straight for the camera/viewer along the z-axis. The ensuing match cut dissolve between this set of crashing waves and Collinwood at night creates a subtle blur between the ocean, with its connotations of fate and inevitability, and the halls of the Great House. Rob-

Title sequence: shots of crashing waves dissolve to an exterior shot of the Great House at Collinwood, suggesting mystery, fate, and a timeless relationship to powerful (super)nature.

ert Cobert's eerie sixteen-note "Dark Shadows" signature theme makes the title sequence even more distinctive and memorable.

After the title sequence, the scene from the teaser usually resumes, and the remainder of each episode is divided by commercial breaks into three or four "acts." Long takes and pans capture the action and dialogue in medium shots and close-ups, and cutting between the three on-set video cameras simulates other classical Hollywood editing tropes, such as shot-reverse shot structures and matches on action. To guide viewer comprehension, a switch in scene within one of the acts is usually accompanied by an exterior reestablishing shot (of the new location) or else is accomplished via a slow dissolve as per classical Hollywood continuity editing. As is common to episodic soap opera narrative form, each of the acts builds to a small climax, with the largest climax reserved for the end of the final act to create a cliff-hanger effect. Cliff-hanger scenes on *Dark Shadows* sometimes propel the narrative with important information, but just as regularly they seem to have been created to end each episode on a moment of fright (or special effect) that contributes more to sensation and character development than to plot. After the episode's final act quickly fades to black, lengthier end credits roll over a shot of one of that day's empty sets, unless the diegetic action has run overtime necessitating an abbreviated credit sequence. Often a studio voice-over announcer would use this airtime to exhort viewers to watch other ABC shows, including the similarly themed *Bewitched*. Typically, the final credits end with an on-screen credit and voice-over announcing that "*Dark Shadows* is a Dan Curtis Production." In all, the narrative action of each episode accounts for approximately twenty-one to twenty-two minutes of the show's thirty-minute total running time, with commercials accounting for the rest.

Most of these daily narrative elements can be exemplified by almost any randomly chosen episode. For example, the final scene of episode 224 (numbered according to the MPI DVD releases), which occurs early in the first Barnabas narrative, ends with David Collins becoming trapped in the Old House where Barnabas has taken up residence. David has come to explore his favorite haunt, when doors mysteriously slam shut and wolves begin to howl in the neighborhood. In a medium to long shot, David wanders nervously around the drawing room set, and as the howling reaches a crescendo, the camera zooms in to a close-up of his terrified face. A musical stinger punctuates the feeling of imminent danger, and a fade to black occurs before the final credits run. The next episode begins with the same bit of narrative action played over again. After the voice-over introduction spoken by Victoria Winters ("Sunset at Collinwood, and the coldness of night settles in . . ."), we again see David trapped in the Old House. As before, he pounds on sealed doors, hears the wolves howl, and expresses fear as he searches the drawing room. Then, as the howls suddenly stop, David runs directly into Barnabas. A musical stinger accompanies a low-angle close-up of a smirking Barnabas, lit from below, and the scene fades to black. When we return to the scene after the title sequence, a more level two-shot of Barnabas and David fills the screen, although Robert Cobert's tremulous music still connotes an uneasy state. Barnabas is now less menacing and more polite as he helps David open the door, which he assures David was just stuck. In this way, story events that might happen in a few minutes of "real time" could be and regularly were stretched out over several days.

Similarly, the cliff-hanger ending of episode 225 is repeated as the teaser of episode 226. In both versions, Maggie Evans, under Barnabas's influence, suffers a nightmare in which she sees herself in a coffin, presumably dead or made into a vampire. In the dream, Maggie's face is replaced with a skull, and Maggie wakes up screaming as the episode ends. (Episodes often ended in climactic dream sequences because they were good places to exploit special effects and shocking visuals without necessarily causing disruption to the overall "waking" narrative.) But just

41

as the Barnabas/David scene was slightly extended the second time it was replayed as the next episode's teaser (recall that the cliff-hanger of episode 224 ended before Barnabas appeared on camera), so too is Maggie's nightmare scene extended when it appears as the next day's teaser: after screaming, Maggie composes herself enough to call her boyfriend, Joe Haskell, on the telephone. In both cases, this extends/expands the cliff-hanger scene via the addition of a new character who was not in the cast of the previous episode (Barnabas or Joe). In fact, the writers were extremely economical with the number of actors they used in any given episode: the budget specified how many actors the show could employ per week and that usually meant no more than four to six actors/characters appearing on any given episode. Extending the cliff-hanger with a new cast member on the following day helps to hide this fact and produces a smoother transition between different episodes (and different casts).

As has been noted repeatedly, the endless repetition of story events by characters within the diegesis is a key trait of soap opera narrative form. Michael Newman suggests that often these repetitive "beats consist of reactions rather than actions," in order to further character development and the audience's emotional involvement ("Beats to Arcs," 18). As Tania Modleski put it in her seminal account of the soap opera, the "script writers, anticipating the housewife's distracted state, are careful to repeat important elements of the story several times" (*Loving*, 102). Indeed, according to *Dark Shadows*' unit manager Michael Brockman, in that pre-VCR/DVR era, it was assumed that the average soap opera viewer would see any given series only twice a week, in effect missing 60 percent of the overall narrative ("Interview"). This necessitated a high level of repetition and reiteration of important narrative events, both within and between episodes. For example, in episode 225, a scene follows the teaser between Barnabas and David wherein they discuss what has just happened, Barnabas slyly denying the supernatu-

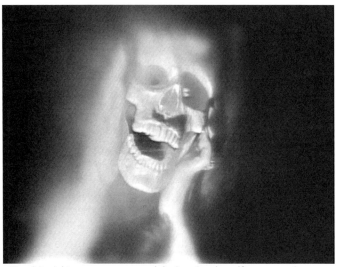

Maggie's nightmare goes awry, and she imagines herself as a screaming skull.

ral cause of the mysterious events in order to soothe a nervous David. Similarly, in episode 226 after the teaser in which Maggie (re)experiences her dream, she describes it for Joe throughout much of the first act. Reiteration is also observed in the immediate postcommercial dialogue beginning each subsequent act, which usually recaps (in one line or two) what has happened in the previous act. It can also be seen across entire episodes as characters not involved with a particular story line sit around the drawing room and discuss what is happening to whom.

Compared to one another, soap operas tend to be either more quickly or slowly plotted. Although *Dark Shadows* exhibited a certain narrative "slowness" in its first year or so, by the time it hit its supernatural stride with the Laura and Barnabas story lines, it became more quickly paced. If *Dark Shadows* fans were indeed more compulsive about watching the show than were average soap opera viewers—and there is good evidence to support that assertion—then its writers may have felt less need to rehash plot points and kept things moving at a faster pace. By the 1897 sequence, *Dark Shadows* was regularly working two distinct but related narrative strands (A and B story lines) into single episodes. However, this narrative strategy may have eventually backfired for the show's producers. In its final years, as the show began simultaneously juggling different historical eras and Parallel Time zones, many fans felt the story became difficult to follow. Some have speculated that this is one of the reasons that led to show's waning ratings share and its ultimate cancellation (Scott, *Companion,* 166).

Six episodes from the introduction of Barnabas story line, episodes that originally aired from Friday to Friday (April 21–28, 1967), more fully describe the narrative flow and formal style of the show during one of its most formative periods. In these episodes (numbered 214–19 on the MPI DVD release), Barnabas arrives at Collinwood and introduces himself as a long-lost ancestor from the English branch of the Collins family. In episode 214, Barnabas meets Carolyn and Roger (having already met Victoria and Elizabeth in episode 211), and in episode 218, Barnabas asks Roger and Elizabeth if he might take up residence at the Old House. The other episodes of this run center on Willie's reappearance in town: he has been missing since he opened a coffin in a secret room of the Collins family mausoleum and was attacked by an offscreen assailant (in episode 210). Everyone is amazed by the strange changes in his personality. As Victoria and Carolyn concur in episode 217, "It's almost as if he's become another person—an entirely different person." During his first few weeks on the show, Willie was played as a brash, abrasive, petty thug, full of sneering bravado and aggressive body language. When Willie reappears at the local bar the Blue Whale in episode 215, he is a totally transformed man. These and subsequent episodes strongly suggest that Willie has been bitten on the wrist by Barnabas, and that this attack is what has caused his extreme personality overhaul.

Yet the episodes mostly hint at these connections between Barnabas and Willie rather than state them (or show them) outright, maintaining a sense of uncertainty common to the gothic genre. For example, in episode 215, when Joe recalls the story of his uncle's calf that was found drained of blood, the camera cuts directly to Willie sitting on the other side of the bar, where it is discovered he has blood on his jacket. The cut suggests Willie has some connection to the drained calf—perhaps having been involved in its death—and/or that the calf and Willie have shared a similar fate (i.e., attack by a vampire). In episode 217, as Willie suffers from the wound on his wrist, a pan to an open bedroom window suggests the generic iconography of the vampire's nocturnal visitation—the so-called beast in the boudoir motif—a staple trope of the classical Hollywood horror film as well as *Dark Shadows* (Greenberg, "*King Kong*"). A bit later in the same episode, Willie sees the portrait of (historic 1795 ancestor) Barnabas in the foyer and hears the sound of a heartbeat. He speaks to the portrait: "I hear ya' callin' me. I hear, and I'm comin'." Willie hurries to the secret room in the mausoleum, yet we never see him actually interact with Barnabas in a coffin. Indeed, even as that cliff-hanger is repeated at the start of episode 218, Barnabas is seen emerging from *around the back* of the mausoleum, not from the secret room, suggesting that Barnabas Collins (cousin from England) is perhaps *not* the same being as the ancient vampire released from his tomb.

These episodes use the doppelgänger theme in a very pronounced way, chiefly as they refuse to confirm that Barnabas is actually the creature we saw reach out from the coffin in episode 210. Instead, it is the subtle mise-en-scène that repeatedly ties together Barnabas the undead vampire and Barnabas the cousin from England, especially via the portrait of Barnabas that hangs prominently in the foyer of the Great House. For example, a match cut dissolve from that portrait to a shot of Barnabas standing in the woods ends episode 214 and strongly suggests *but does not confirm* that these three representations/ avatars of Barnabas are really one and the same.

Stylistically, these six episodes also exemplify the show's usual visual style in terms of sets, costumes, and lighting. The plush interiors of the Great House and the cobwebbed ruins of the Old House are both shot on black-and-white video, although the former tends to be more brightly lit than the latter. (Within the diegesis, even after it is restored to its 1795 grandeur, the Old House is supposedly only ever illuminated with candles in order to preserve its "old-world charm" and more gothic feel.) Key lighting effects create both obvious shad-

A matching dissolve from the eighteenth-century portrait of Barnabas Collins to present-day "Cousin Barnabas" suggests—but does not prove—that both men are one and the same.

ows as well as more subtle visual effects, especially at the Old House or during assorted uncanny moments. Lamps placed near the floor of the studio are frequently used to illuminate the actors and sets from below, adding a disquieting feeling to many scenes. Scenes at the Blue Whale bar are enhanced with a reflected shimmering light effect meant to invoke the play of light on the water that supposedly lies outside the waterfront dive.

The costumes for these sequences are both functional and symbolic. Thus, while Roger and Carolyn wear fashionable clothes of the era, Elizabeth and Jason wear black—she because of her morbid attachment to the estate and Jason to connote his villainy. (Jason—formerly Willie's boss in various shady deals—is blackmailing Elizabeth over knowledge of her former husband's fate.) Barnabas's costume, one that quickly became iconic for the character, is an interesting update of previous cinematic vampire wear. A dark gray form-fitting double-breasted suit and tie suggests both bygone eras as well as a touch of mid-1960s Carnaby Street mod. (Where Willie shopped for this outfit in Collinsport is never revealed!) Barnabas's dark-jeweled ring, silver wolf's head cane, and short cape-jacket complete his look as an elegant modern-day vampire with nostalgic touches. Barnabas also wears a gray fedora in some of his earliest appearances, a fashion choice that was soon dropped in order to showcase a more stylized haircut with carefully coiffed spiky "Roman" bangs.

Framing and editing are consistent with the era's televisual soap opera style as discussed above. Most of these episodes use a combination of middle-range two-shots and shot-reverse shot structures for conversation scenes; however, more complexly framed shots are also used to comment on the action. Thus, in episode 219, as Victoria and Carolyn stand in the foyer and discuss the mystery of what has happened to Willie, they are pointedly framed on either side of the portrait of Barnabas. The characters may remain clueless, but the framing suggests

47

the preferred reading: Barnabas is what has happened to Willie. Close-ups are used during conversation scenes but are also central to "window" shots in which characters are shot from "exterior" angles, the window framing their faces to add emphasis and emotion. Similar to the window number in musical films (wherein a given character sings out his or her heart's desire while perched on the window sill), window shots in *Dark Shadows* emphasize paradigmatic character development over syntagmatic flow. Similar close-ups, accompanied by musical stingers and fades to black, almost always end each act. A particularly striking example of such a close-up occurs in the middle of episode 214 as Barnabas and Victoria examine the decaying Old House. Comparing the Old House to the pyramids, Vicky comments that unlike the pyramids, the Old House was not built to be a tomb. Barnabas replies (with much ironic inflection) that that is true: "The house was never *designed* to be a tomb." As he turns away from Vicky, he is framed in close-up between the upright supports of the staircase, a visual that suggests that the Old House is Barnabas's prison as well as his tomb.

Interestingly, even when Barnabas is not in a given episode, the mise-en-scène still works to recall him, not only through his portrait in the foyer, but also via the now-stricken Willie. In episode 216, Jason insists on bringing Willie back to Collinwood, only to have him see the portrait, scream, and drop into a dead faint. Once Willie is put to bed upstairs, Jason himself seems to suggest the offscreen and unnamed vampiric attack: Jason wears black clothing and hovers over Willie's bed to interrogate him. In addition, an offscreen lighting source from below and to the side of the bed creates an uneasy feeling, almost suggesting a vampiric attack from Jason-cum-Barnabas. These character and shot dynamics also give rise to a homoerotic reading: Willie has been Jason's second-in-command/roommate/traveling buddy, and he is now becoming all of that (and more) to Barnabas. True to the gendered and sexualized

Under-lighting and low-angle mise-en-scène trap Barnabas within the "bars" of the staircase, a cinematographic touch that would not be out of place in a Hollywood melodrama by Douglas Sirk.

dynamics of *Dracula* and vampire films in general, it is easy to read Barnabas's attack on Willie as a sexualized one, which is perhaps why it occurred offscreen and on Willie's wrist, in effect blunting that potential reading. Still, Willie has been left a shattered man by his homoerotic encounter with Barnabas, not an entranced lover, as most of Barnabas's female victims will soon be. Willie is yet another example of an ongoing hysterical male character on the show, made even more so by the histrionic way he is played by actor John Karlen.

Actor, Character, Narrative

As many prominent theorists of television aesthetics have noted, "Personality is one of the primary selling points of television, the basis of its performers' appeal" (Joyrich, "Television," 138). Dorothy Hobson states simply that "actors in soap operas, and the characters they portray, are the main attractions that bring audiences to the genre" (*Soap Opera*, 67). Similarly, David Thorburn argues that "far more decisively than the movie-actor, the television-actor creates and controls the meaning of what we see on the screen" ("Melodrama," 631). Thorburn also suggests that all television melodrama is bigger than life and *operatic;* as such, it offers yet another textual pleasure: "the brilliant individual performance" (ibid., 634). Indeed, *Dark Shadows* would be considerably less engaging if it were not for its stock company of energetic and highly theatrical performers. Their theatrical excesses further the links between the quotidian and the supernatural, an important point of Helen Wheatley's book *Gothic Television*. Speaking about *Dark Shadows* directly, she notes that "emotional excess is also located in performance in *Dark Shadows,* in which the actors produce a kind of hybrid performance style which combines daytime drama convention with a more theatrical heritage of Gothic performance" (153).

Thus, the acting on *Dark Shadows* is very different from the acting on so-called normal soap operas, whether from the 1960s or the 2000s. Its performance style directly contradicts Dorothy Hobson's broad assertion that "for the most part, actors in soap operas have to produce performances that are understated and low key, always less than 'actorly,' for it is their job to create the illusion of the ordinary" (*Soap Opera,* 67). Granted, Hobson was writing about realistic British serials like *Crossroads* (1964–88) and *EastEnders* (1985–) when she made that comment, but the actors on *Dark Shadows* are more regularly known for calling attention to their theatrical excess than for any form of realistic or naturalistic acting, however modulated by televisual form. Supernatural characters seemed to demand supernatural performance styles, and *Dark Shadows*' actors delivered those in abundance. Nevertheless, the writers and actors still created characters who—although they did not and could not exist in the "real" world—had identifiable and understandable problems, allowing audiences to "satisfy their desires for knowledge about [them] and for forging an emotional connection with them" (Newman, "Beats to Arcs," 17).

The actors on *Dark Shadows* functioned almost as a repertory company: many of them played several roles throughout the course of the show's five-year run. While the "long-lost twin" story line may be a staple of more "normal" soap operas, *Dark Shadows* stretched that trope to extreme dimensions. In different time periods, actors doubled for their ancestors or played Parallel Time selves, and some actors even played different characters within the same time period. This blur between the actor and his or her multiple roles on the show foregrounds issues of performance and is a self-reflexive technique perhaps more common to metatextual modernist texts than vulgar art forms like the soap opera. Because of this trope (as well as the show's preponderance of technical gaffes and blown lines), audience members are often acutely aware that they are watching a performance as well as a fictional scene. It is perhaps harder to "suspend disbelief" and immerse oneself in the diegesis when the characters are reflexively calling attention to themselves as actors. The opening voice-over narration (after Victoria Winters left the show) also adds to this effect: as different cast members began to speak the opening monologue, they were never identified as their characters per se, which raises the question of who was speaking, the actor or the character. True to the gothic form in general, this odd amalgamation of character and actor in one narrational voice, along with the show's obsession with doubles, mirrors, doppelgängers, haunted portraits, spiritual possessions, and secret selves, foregrounds a deeply decentered subjectivity.

Many of the show's key character/actor complexes also embody specific narrative functions, such as investigator, ingenue, and/or supervillain. These functions take on added resonance when compared across different historical eras or Parallel Time zones. Some actors play similar roles no matter what, lending some consistency to the characters they play, despite their changing environs. Others play vastly different roles in different eras or time zones, creating a further sense of irony and distance about them. Some character/actor complexes are replete with extensive intertextual references to previous roles and the actors' real-life personas, while others are relatively free of such extratextual "baggage." In order to exemplify the show's unique form in regard to performance (as well as help familiarize the uninitiated with the major figures of the show), some examples of these actor/character complexes are discussed below.

Alexandra Moltke played Victoria Winters, who was the original "engine" of the narrative, designed to be the "normal" gothic ingenue who discovers the mysteries of Collinwood. Young, petite, and pretty, Alexandra Moltke was one of the few central actors on the show who did not play multiple roles or even undergo significant personality shifts via spells or possessions. For the first few years of the show, it is Victoria who literally narrates the saga as she speaks each episode's opening monologue. Victoria furthers the plot by perkily asking questions, opening closet doors, and uncovering family secrets. When the show shifted its narrative to 1795 via a time-traveling séance, it was twentieth-century Victoria who encountered a new cast of characters (and thus introduced them to twentieth-century audiences). Throughout her tenure at Collinwood, Victoria also served as a generic love object and/or victim of vampiric attentions. In fact, once Barnabas was introduced and other investigator figures (such as Dr. Julia Hoffman) appeared, Victoria became increasingly superfluous to the narrative, a fact that disturbed actress Moltke. In an interview from 1968, Moltke complained, "Victoria is so dumb . . . all I do is stand around saying 'I don't understand what's happening'" (quoted in Fox, "Vampire," 81). She may have started out as a sort of "Nancy Drew, Girl Investigator," but Victoria was increasingly written as bewildered rather than proactive. After asking to be cast in different types of roles (and being denied), Moltke was released from her contract when she became pregnant in 1968.

There is one other extratextual tidbit important to the Alexandra Moltke/Victoria Winters actor/character complex, one that most latter-day fans of the show continue to speak of in relation to the fictional intrigues at Collinwood. In 1982, long after she left *Dark Shadows*, Alexandra Moltke was subpoenaed to take the stand in the sensational murder trial of Claus von Bulow, a wealthy New York socialite accused of injecting insulin into his wife, Sunny, resulting in an irreversible coma. Moltke was revealed to be the "other woman" in von Bulow's life, the mistress for whom he had allegedly attempted murder. Von Bulow was found guilty, although a second trial reversed that decision. Many latter-day viewers of *Dark Shadows* cannot help but compare Moltke's "real-life" events to the various trials for witchcraft that Victoria Winters was forced to endure in 1795. In the 1990s, Moltke became a documentary filmmaker specializing in topics related to Jewish history, including the Holocaust and the blacklist, for the most part distancing herself from *Dark Shadows* and its ongoing fandoms.

Joan Bennett played Elizabeth Collins Stoddard, the undisputed matriarch of Collinwood. Cast for her classical Hollywood star status and upper-crust matronly manner, Bennett also brought gothic/noir intertextuality to her *Dark Shadows* roles, having starred in several such Hollywood films directed by Fritz Lang, including *The Woman in the Window* (1943), *Scarlet Street* (1945), and *Secret Beyond the Door* (1948). Like Alexandra Moltke, Joan Bennett was also part of a real-life scandal that contributes to her various on-screen *Dark Shadows* personae. In 1951, her then husband Walter Wanger shot and wounded her agent, Jennings Lang, because he thought Lang was having an affair with Bennett. On *Dark Shadows,* Bennett never played supernatural characters per se, but several of her characters *were* involved in murderous love triangles, echoing her real-life story. In 1967, Elizabeth thinks she is hiding her husband's murdered body in the basement, and in 1897, Bennett as Judith Collins has her unscrupulous and cheating husband Reverend Trask walled up alive in the West Wing. After leaving *Dark Shadows,* Bennett finally did get a chance to play a supernatural figure: she leads a coven of witches in Italian horror auteur Dario Argento's stylish thriller *Suspiria* (1977).

Although Bennett played multiple roles on the show, her various characters rarely strayed far from her original persona as Elizabeth Collins Stoddard. In 1795 she played Naomi Collins, head of the household and mother to Barnabas. In the 1897 sequence, Bennett was Judith Collins, again running the estate while falling afoul of several nefarious plots. Sometimes neurotic, alcoholic, or flighty, Bennett's characters also frequently displayed strength and determination as she struggled to keep her family together. Especially during the first year of the show, Bennett's Elizabeth Collins Stoddard might be understood as a rather generic soap opera mother, a sturdy trunk around whom various family intrigues entwine. She also seems to run the family business (fishing and canning) with more efficiency than does her brother Roger. However, after the introduction of Barnabas, Bennett's characters arguably became more peripheral. (They also increasingly suffered from collapses that resulted in off camera hospital stays, allowing the actress generous time off for other projects.) Bennett's characters began to function more and more as a type of narrative "negation." Denying or choosing not to see the supernatural events around them, Bennett's characters often look and act as if they are on tranquilizers, wandering around Collinwood dully intoning lines like "I'd rather not talk about it." In this way, Bennett's characters' repeated denials work to arouse even further curiosity from the audience.

The matriarch of Collinwood, Elizabeth Collins Stoddard (former Hollywood star Joan Bennett), and her rather snobbish brother, Roger Collins (the effete Louis Edmonds).

Louis Edmonds's portrayal of Roger Collins is another excellent example of how a performer and his or her roles can and did mesh during the run of the show. In most of the show's varied story arcs, Louis Edmonds plays a rather ineffectual father. His marriages fail, his sons become vampires or try to kill him, and he is usually overshadowed by his wife or sister, often played by Joan Bennett. Even when Edmonds played stern patriarch Joshua Collins in the 1795 sequence, he was still at the mercy of the witch Angelique, who turned him into a cat for a few episodes. However, Louis Edmonds is probably remembered most fondly for playing Roger Collins during the show's contemporary sequences. Haughty and sneering, Roger Collins is constantly sipping brandy in the drawing room and making bitchy bon mots about his family and friends. Like his sister, Elizabeth, Roger is prone to dismiss the supernatural events occurring all around him, until they grow too prominent to be ignored. However, while Roger might be concerned about the welfare of his son David or his niece Carolyn, he is usually unable to battle the supernatural threats that besiege the family himself, that task being more readily performed by Barnabas, Julia, and/or Professor Stokes.

One of the many gay actors on the show, Louisiana-born Louis Edmonds brought Southern charm, dapper good looks, and dissolute irony to his role as Roger Collins, a tactic that invites spectators to read the show in equally ironic, vaguely dismissive terms. David Henesy, the child actor who played Roger's son, later recalled Edmonds's queer appeal when he described him as "a Tennessee Williams character, in the flesh" (quoted in Hamrick, *Big Lou,* vii). Perhaps because of his eloquent queer persona, Louis Edmonds never achieved much acting success outside of New York City's theaters and soundstages. Aside from the film *House of Dark Shadows,* Edmonds's only other Hollywood film credit is the rarely seen Troy Donahue vehicle *Come Spy with Me* (1967). Eventually Louis Edmonds found success as a character actor on another soap opera playing conman turned lovable rapscallion Langley Wallingford on *All My Children* (1970–).

Jonathan Frid as Barnabas Collins was *the* iconic actor/character of *Dark Shadows* and became the center of a media frenzy during the run of the show, even appearing at a children's party at the Nixon White House. Barnabas was originally written as a forthright monster—brutally beating his manservant Willie Loomis and cold-bloodedly murdering others—but over the years he softened into a more reluctant gothic hero, occasionally even cured of his vampirism. A Shakespearean-trained actor from Canada with an MFA in directing from the Yale School of Drama, Frid nonetheless had a terrible time learning all of his lines, and he frequently forgot them on camera, all the while stammering and stuttering to make sense of them. Despite that, many fans found this trait either endearing or in character with the out-of-place-and-time vampire. To his surprise, Frid also became a major sex symbol during the run of the show, an honor with which the actor was never comfortable. During his public appearances, he was often mobbed by women and children, and he once told an interviewer that "I always feel like an ass being a teenage idol in a teeny-bopper magazine" (quoted in Hamrick, *Barnabas*, 7). Toward the end of the show's five-year run, in the Parallel Time 1841 story line, Frid played Bramwell Collins, a "normal" character based on Heathcliff from *Wuthering Heights*. This toothless role arguably hastened the cancellation of the show, and fans remember Frid best as the suave and charming vampire Barnabas Collins.

Importantly, Barnabas was at the center of the show's most intense romantic couplings. His love for Josette DuPres, which was first explored in depth in the 1795 story arc, permeates the entire series, as Barnabas searches for her (or some reincarnated form of her) throughout time and space. His relationship with the witch Angelique, who was responsible for placing the curse of vampirism on him, is also a major love-hate relationship that anchors the serial. Sometimes Barnabas and Angelique are totally at odds with each other; at other times they are reluctantly forced to cooperate in order to defeat some larger threat. Dr. Julia Hoffman, who also loves Barnabas, was first brought on the show to expose and destroy him, but she later mellowed into his adoring accomplice. Arguably, their platonic relationship resonated even more with fans than did the Barnabas/Josette or Barnabas/Angelique relationships. After the actress who played Josette left the show, Barnabas shifted his attentions to another of the show's generic ingenue characters, Roxanne Drew (Donna Wandrey), but their relationship was a relatively brief one within the show's five-year run.

Frid often described his approach to playing Barnabas as not simply embodying a monster but playing him as a sort of tragic Shakespearean figure, "a man with a hang up." When asked about Barnabas's appeal on *The Merv Griffin Show* (in 1969 during the height of the show's popularity), Frid suggested it was "the bite," but also played coy, saying he did not "want to get into Freudian psychology" and the sexual implications that those theories would suggest. In the same interview, Frid allowed that "maybe people sympathize with the fact that he's got something to fight." These comments are especially provocative in light of the long-standing rumors that Frid himself was gay but was forced by producer Dan Curtis to stay in the closet so as not to ruin Barnabas's (hetero)sexual appeal. If Frid was gay but closeted, perhaps he used that situation to nuance Barnabas's "fight" against his vampiric urges, a subtext many fans have discerned over the years. Perhaps not wishing to suffer the media's inquiries about his private life for the rest of his career, Frid made only two films after *House of Dark Shadows*: the television movie *The Devil's Daughter* (1973) and Oliver Stone's little-seen cult horror film *Seizure* (1974). Instead, Frid went back to his theatrical roots and in recent years has begun to renew his participation with the *Dark Shadows* fan community, making a few convention appearances and interacting with fans on his website, www.jonathanfrid.com.

Kathryn Leigh Scott first appeared on the show as Maggie Evans, a brassy, wisecracking waitress at the Collinsport Inn. She soon mellowed into a more typically pretty and demure ingenue figure and became the first object of Barnabas's romantic/vampiric seductions when Barnabas kidnapped her and attempted to turn her into his long-lost lover, Josette DuPres. As noted above, the Barnabas/Josette coupling became one of the show's central romantic anchors, with Barnabas seeing some form of reincarnated Josette in just about every character Kathryn Leigh Scott played on the show, including Rachel Drummond and Lady Kitty Soames, both in the 1897 sequence. Maggie also was married to Quentin in the 1970 Parallel Time sequence, but unlike some of the other actors' highly variable roles, Scott's persona did not change much from one ingenue to another. Further underlining her generic narrative function, once Alexandra Moltke/Victoria Winters left the show, Maggie moved into the Great House at Collinwood to be the new governess, as well as to be closer to the mysterious goings-on.

Scott had studied acting and performed in local theater, but *Dark Shadows* was her first professional job. She was working as a Playboy Bunny when Dan Curtis hired her for *Dark Shadows,* which perhaps indicates that Curtis was looking for someone with more sex appeal than acting credentials. Nonetheless, Scott's unproven theatrical talents fit with the rest of the cast's over-the-top performance aesthetics. During the run of the show, Scott became very close friends with Joel Crothers (another actor rumored to be gay), even as they were occasionally linked up romantically on-screen. Following *Dark Shadows*' official demise, Scott acted sporadically on television, and in the late 1980s she founded Pomegranate Press, a boutique publishing company that specializes in entertainment-themed books, including several by Scott herself such as *My Scrapbook Memories of "Dark Shadows."* Gracious and charming, Kathryn Leigh Scott remains very active in *Dark Shadows* fandoms.

Lara Parker was the vengeful witch Angelique, a beautiful

and fiery blonde dynamo with an evil cackle that fans still ask Parker to perform at *Dark Shadows* conventions. Angelique was first introduced during the 1795 sequence as part of Barnabas's origin narrative, employed as Josette DuPres' maid. As the story unfolds, it is revealed that Barnabas and Angelique had had a brief fling, before his proposal of marriage to Josette. Jealous of Josette and desirous of Barnabas for herself, Angelique uses witchcraft to cause mayhem at Collinwood and eventually places the curse of vampirism on Barnabas. With her spells and talismans, Angelique was a very powerful force on the show, even as most of her actions were driven by her spite for Barnabas. In present-day 1968, Lara Parker appeared as Roger's new wife Cassandra, another witch who is eventually revealed to be Angelique herself. This time, however, her powers are somewhat mitigated by the warlock Nicholas Blair, who turns her briefly into a vampire for a run of episodes.

61

A supernatural variation on the spurned-lover-out-for-revenge stock character, Angelique was a thorn in Barnabas's side (and now and then Quentin's) during most of the show's run. However, circumstances sometimes made uneasy allies of the enemies, as when all three teamed up to battle Count Petofi in the 1897 sequence. Like her gothic male counterparts, Angelique did evil things, but her motivations were always understandable and often justified. In various Parallel Time sequences near the end of the show's run, Lara Parker played the dual role of twins Angelique and Alexis Stokes, as well as more generic non-supernatural parts. Although Parker acted in numerous films and television shows after *Dark Shadows,* major stardom eluded her. She remains active in the *Dark Shadows* fan community and is the author of *Angelique's Descent,* a two-part novel that explores her most famous character's life before and after her fateful meeting with Barnabas Collins.

Grayson Hall played Dr. Julia Hoffman, who was brought on *Dark Shadows* first to investigate and then subsequently attempt to cure Barnabas of his vampirism. In the process she became one of the most important characters on show. Allegedly, the role of Dr. Julia Hoffman had been written for a man until a typographical error misplaced the *n* on the end of his first name. Julia was yet another strong-willed professional female character on the show, even as her unrequited love for Barnabas often drove her support for and protection of him (even while he chased other younger women). Aside from her narrative role as investigator and helpmate to Barnabas, Julia also functions in the narrative as an endless source of hermeneutic delay and repetition. One of her signature lines, spoken in tentative, leading tones, was "You mean . . . ," thus allowing another character to restate a bit more of the story and flesh out each episode. Julia was also fond of offering sedatives whenever anyone approached hysteria, yet another way to slow down the story line. Though a "normal" person, Julia's medical powers (she performs several mad laboratory narratives during the series) and her power to hypnotize people with a colorfully bejeweled amulet link her to Collinwood's supernatural figures, blurring the line between normality and the monstrous within her very character.

Before *Dark Shadows,* Grayson Hall was best known for her Oscar-nominated role as a crypto-lesbian schoolteacher in the film version of Tennessee Williams's *Night of the Iguana* (1964). That fact, along with her over-the-top, take-no-prisoners acting style endeared her to many fans who appreciated Grayson Hall/Julia Hoffman as primarily a camp diva. As one critic (rather delicately) puts it, "Like all of the actors on the show, Grayson was directed to play her lines to the hilt—as if she was on stage instead of just a few feet from the camera" (Hamrick, *Barnabas,* 5). Even in the 1980s, as the series was being rediscovered via its PBS airings, a critic for the *Village Voice* described Grayson Hall's acting style as one in which she "registers 16 facial expressions per emotion" (quoted in ibid., 13). One of her most memorable over-the-top moments in the entire series occurs in 1968 when Dr. Hoffman experiences Angelique's (allegedly terrifying) "Dream Curse": with little-to-no dialogue during several minutes of screen time, Hall/Hoffman mugs and screams and gasps at various cheesy special effects meant to drive her into madness before breaking down into a long, sobbing "No-oo-oo-oo-oooooo!"

Adding to her metatextual actor/character appeal, Grayson Hall also chewed up the *Dark Shadows* scenery playing several other memorable parts. As Josette's Aunt Natalie DuPres in the 1795 sequences, she read tarot cards and predicted disaster while twittering in a faux French accent. As the gypsy Magda in 1897, she wore dark pancake makeup, lots of clanking jewelry, and was given to broad exasperated gestures and exclamations. ("Baaaaah!") As both Magda and Julia were essentially helpmates to Barnabas, this casting also set up intratextual points of comparison. In Parallel Time 1970, Grayson Hall reigned in her mannered style (somewhat) to play a coldly calculating housekeeper known simply as "Hoffman," based on Mrs. Danvers from *Rebecca* (1940), yet another crypto-lesbian character in the gothic-romantic tradition. After *Dark Shadows*, Grayson Hall—who was married to the show's head writer Sam Hall—worked mostly in television and theater until her death in 1985.

John Karlen, who played Willie Loomis, seems to have based his performance as the vampire's servant on Dwight Frye's Renfield in the original film version of *Dracula* (1931). Like that actor, Karlen imbues the vampire's manservant with a nervous, slightly crazed energy that always seems about to tip over into camp. John Karlen was not shy about twitching his mouth, rolling his eyes, moaning aloud, and/or generally breaking down into a heap of slobbering nerves whenever confronted by the show's various horrors, including Barnabas (at least during his first months on the show). Nonetheless, as Barnabas transitioned from bloodthirsty to reluctant vampire, so too did Willie regain some of his composure and ethics; his desires for the young women of Collinsport led him to try to protect them

63

on several occasions. As the series progressed, Willie and Julia took care of Barnabas and protected his secret(s) at all costs. In the 1897 story line, John Karlen was also dangerously close to over-the-top as Carl Collins, a foolish giggling boob who loves practical jokes. In other sequences, Karlen played less-neurotic Collins men, although his Desmond Collins in the 1840 sequence is responsible for unleashing further terror at Collinwood via the disembodied head of warlock Judah Zachary.

Brooklyn-born John Karlen had studied acting at New York's Academy of Dramatic Arts and worked both on Broadway and in television during the early 1960s. After *Dark Shadows,* he parlayed his success as Willie Loomis into several other horror film projects, including the cult lesbian vampire film *Daughters of Darkness* (1971) and Dan Curtis's television versions of *Frankenstein* (1973) and *The Picture of Dorian Gray* (1973).

Cringing, sniveling, stuttering, and blubbering: often on the verge of hysteria, Barnabas's manservant Willie was played by John Karlen.

Karlen also had a long-running part on *Cagney & Lacey* (CBS, 1982–88), winning an Emmy Award playing husband to Tyne Daly's Detective Mary Beth Lacey. Karlen remains active in *Dark Shadows* fan culture and is usually willing to laugh along with the crowd at some of the show's more outlandish excesses (including his own).

Thayer David played Professor T. Eliot Stokes, a master of arcane knowledge, and he helps to narrate some of the present-day *Dark Shadows* story lines in which he appears almost directly, explaining supernatural events and paranormal phenomena such as the I-Ching or Parallel Time. A sort of less-vindictive Professor Van Helsing character adorned with smoking jacket and monocle, Timothy Eliot Stokes often aids Julia Hoffman and Barnabas as they investigate the latest uncanny phenomena occurring at Collinwood. Out of all the actors on the show, Thayer David played the most—and the most varied range of—characters, from supervillain to menial servant. Even before Barnabas appeared on the show, David played a surly groundskeeper at Collinwood named Matthew Morgan, who briefly kidnapped Victoria Winters until the ghost of Josette came to her rescue. In 1795, he played Ben Stokes, Barnabas's faithful servant.

In the 1897 sequence, David played two major roles. As the slow-witted gypsy Sandor opposite Grayson Hall's Magda, David sputtered and cowered beneath his dark wig and floppy glue-on mustache. As the supervillain Count Andreas Petofi (a powerful magician/warlock modeled on Count Saint-Germain, a medieval alchemist who had sought eternal life), David wore a tightly kinked gray wig and purple John Lennon granny-glasses. A sort of evil version of Professor Stokes, Count Petofi was a sophisticated man of eloquent words and elaborate plans. Aided and abetted by his pretty-boy assistant Aristede (Michael Stroka), Petofi comes to Collinwood to reclaim his missing hand—severed by the gypsies—and hatches various plans to take over the (immortal) bodies of Barnabas and Quentin as a means of escaping the gypsies by traveling into the future. (In one intriguing episode, Count Petofi uses a wooden cabinet to see into the future of Collinwood, a highly self-reflexive gesture since the cabinet—imbued with Petofi's powers—suggests a Victorian-era television set on which yet another series of events at Collinwood are unfolding.)

Before, during, and after *Dark Shadows,* Thayer David was a corpulent and competent character actor with a raspy voice and commanding presence. Educated at Harvard, his erudition informed many of the roles he played. He had a long career onstage, in television, and in films such as *Journey to the Center of the Earth* (1959), *Little Big Man* (1970), *Save the Tiger* (1973), and *Rocky* (1976). One of the first original cast members to pass away (in 1978), David missed much of the ongoing fan adulation that many of the show's other cast members have enjoyed.

Thayer David as archvillain Count Petofi in the 1897 sequence, complete with mod curly wig, glued-on muttonchops, and purple John Lennon glasses.

Nonetheless, David remains an important aspect of the show, not just for his many varied characters, but for the campy and theatrical ways he embodied them.

David Selby as Quentin Collins was brought on the show about halfway through its five-year run to play another supernatural gothic hero (and give some time off to Jonathan Frid). Selby was born in West Virginia and brought a gentle southern drawl to his performance of Quentin Collins. Quentin first appears as a ghost in 1968 and is a central character in the 1897 flashback that was partly devoted to explaining his origins. Tall, handsome, and charming, the human Quentin is a softhearted rogue who likes wealth, women, and wine. Affable and easygoing, Quentin dabbles in the black arts but is more often acted upon by others. For example, in the 1897 sequence, Quentin is first turned into a zombie by Angelique and then turned into a werewolf by the gypsy Magda. Count Petofi also has his ways with Quentin—blinding him, taking over his body and mind, and even strapping him under a giant pendulum blade, as in Edgar Allan Poe's "The Pit and the Pendulum." After the 1897 flashback, Selby appears as a contemporary character named Grant Douglas, but he is soon revealed to be the same immortal Quentin Collins from previous generations. In other narrative sequences Quentin appears as a more "normal" husband and father (albeit one with eternal life).

David Selby as Quentin Collins soon rivaled Frid as Barnabas in popularity, and he also became a pop-cult heartthrob for the teenybopper set. In a canny stylistic touch, Quentin's Edwardian/Victorian look—wavy dark hair and muttonchops—could and did suggest both the nostalgic bygone era of the 1890s as well as the longer, shaggier cuts of young men's hairstyles in the late 1960s. David Selby continues to be a working actor, as well as an activist for leftist causes. He made his movie debut with *Night of Dark Shadows* (1971), the second film based on the soap opera, and then costarred with Barbra Streisand in *Up the Sandbox* (1972). His other long-running television role

67

was playing Richard Channing on the nighttime soap opera *Falcon Crest* (CBS, 1981–90). Like Lara Parker and Kathryn Leigh Scott, David Selby also remains active in *Dark Shadows* fandom.

This discussion of *Dark Shadows*' more charismatic and characteristic actor/character complexes is by the scope of this project necessarily incomplete, but a few other key performers should be mentioned as they too contributed to the show's over-the-top performance mode in multiple ways. For example, Humbert Allen Astredo's wickedly twinkling eyes, rolling *r* sounds, and black mustache as he assayed the roles of warlock Nicholas Blair and occultist Evan Hanley suggested Victorian stage melodrama in its purest form—all that was missing was a black cape and a top hat. Jerry Lacy's various Reverend Trasks were equally villainous, especially as he shouted exorcisms or dragged suspected witches across teetering studio sets. Clarice Blackburn as the Collinses' housekeeper Mrs. Johnson was both meekly subservient and prissily defiant, as were her historical characters. Also memorable was Christopher Pennock, who always gave 110 percent to his roles, whether it was as Leviathan deity Jeb Hawkes, the crippled and bitter Gabriel Collins, hippie astrologer Sebastian Shaw, or the scenery-chewing Cyrus Longworth and John Yaeger (the show's *Dr. Jekyll and Mr. Hyde* characters). Trying to ground all of this madness were the (usually) more subdued performances of actresses like Nancy Barrett, Donna McKechnie, and Kate Jackson, who played various love interests and gothic ingenues. Together, *Dark Shadows*' actors created a unique diegetic space, one that allowed for gothic and romantic frissons as well as more specialized metatextual pleasures based on performance, character, and narrative.

Chapter 6
Cultural Context
Camp, Reception, and Secondary Texts

s its immense popularity suggests, *Dark Shadows* may have been just the right show at just the right cultural moment. In its first years or so on the air, it was considered by some to be reminiscent of the work of Alfred Hitchcock, perhaps because of its suspense and the presence of 1940s Hollywood mystery icon Joan Bennett. Soon however, it was being decoded by many viewers and commentators against the backdrop of the 1960s counterculture and especially via that era's growing appreciation of dissident ideologies, psychedelic aesthetics, and campy irony. Although *Dark Shadows* deliberately ignored the actual day-to-day issues of that very volatile era (political assassinations, race and racism, the ongoing nuclear arms and space race, the war in Vietnam), it did tap into broader countercultural trends of the youth movement, including women's liberation and the search for alternative spiritualities. In one of the few academic papers written on *Dark Shadows* in recent years, Rick Worland argues that the Jeb Hawkes/Leviathan sequence does contain a (conflicted, paranoid) commentary on the era's youth movement, as Jeb literally grows from a demon seed a la *Rosemary's Baby* into some sort of monstrous hippie out to topple his more staid elders at Collinwood ("*Dark Shadows,* 1970").

Just as some sectors of the counterculture were becoming interested in arcane spiritual subject matters like hypnosis, the occult, and the tarot, so too were those major thematic elements on *Dark Shadows*. Specifically, witchcraft as a form of female empowerment and/or resistance to patriarchal Christianity was easily thematized on *Dark Shadows* via the character of Angelique. This trope was common throughout the era and appears in popular texts as varied as the sitcom *Bewitched,* the children's movie *Pufnstuf* (1970), and George A. Romero's *Season of the Witch* (1972; a.k.a. *Jack's Wife* a.k.a. *Hungry Wives*), his follow up to *Night of the Living Dead* (1968). Although actual hallucinogens or hallucinogenic drug trips were never spoken of at Collinwood, the bodies and souls of the Collins family were repeatedly affected by altered states of consciousness and visualized on-screen with swirling colorful special effects that "sometimes looked like small-screen LSD trips" (Hamrick, *Barnabas*, xvii).

Perhaps most importantly, when *Dark Shadows* premiered in 1966, there was a thriving "monster culture" in the United States, a renaissance in horror movie production, popularity, and related ancillary texts (Skal, *Monster Show,* 229–85). This monster culture appealed to both children and young adults, baby boomer consumers who were redefining all aspects of American popular culture. This youthful monster culture arguably began in the mid- to late 1950s, when small film companies like American International Pictures (AIP) "discovered" the niche youth market and exploited it by making and/or distributing low-budget rock-and-roll films, science fiction/horror films, and teenage monster movies. England's Hammer Films contributed to the trend with lush color remakes of classic gothic stories such as *Curse of Frankenstein* (1957), *Horror of Dracula* (1958), *Curse of the Werewolf* (1961), and *The Phantom of the Opera* (1962). In the early 1960s, AIP stalwart Roger Corman switched from black-and-white science fiction films to color widescreen gothic extravaganzas (often starring

Vincent Price) such as *House of Usher* (1960), *Pit and the Pendulum* (1961), *The Haunted Palace* (1963), and *The Tomb of Ligeia* (1964). Many of those films centered on time-tripping or reincarnated spirits out for revenge, as did gothic horror melodramas from Europe such as *Black Sunday* (1960) and *Nightmare Castle* (1965). Even the Hollywood majors got into the game with haunted house stories such as Twentieth Century Fox's *The Innocents* (1961) and MGM's *The Haunting* (1963). As should be apparent, all of these films served in some way as templates for what *Dark Shadows* would try to do just a few years later: adapt classic gothic literature into audiovisual form for a new generation of media-savvy horror fans.

As discussed previously, television too was not immune to horror and/or suspense during these years. Anthology series like *The Twilight Zone* (CBS, 1959–64), *Thriller* (NBC, 1960–62), and *The Outer Limits* (ABC, 1963–65) presented science fiction, fantasy, and horror tales in more or less straightforward ways, but as the decade wore on, "fantastic family sit-coms" like *Bewitched, The Addams Family,* and *The Munsters* turned witches, vampires, Frankenstein monsters, and other assorted supernatural freaks into endearing comic figures and/or metaphorical Others (Spigel, "Domestic Space"). This "burlesquing" of Hollywood's more classical monsters had arguably begun with *Abbott and Costello Meet Frankenstein* (1948) and helped lay the groundwork for the rise of more realist sociopathic monsters like Norman Bates in *Psycho* (1960) or any number of Vincent Price's obsessed madmen. In this context, creating a gothic soap opera about vampires, werewolves, and witches was perhaps not as groundbreaking as it might have otherwise seemed.

Partly, "monster culture" fans were media savvy because of the release to television in 1958 of *Shock Theater,* a package of fifty-two vintage Universal horror films that could be seen in syndication across the United States. More and more older horror films were released to television as other studios followed suit, and the airwaves became awash in older monster movies of varying quality and appeal. These films were often introduced (and commented on) by local television personalities made-up as campy gothic characters: a few of the more famous include Vampira (in the Los Angeles area), Ghoulardi (in Cleveland), and Zacherley (in New York). Top ten pop music hits such as "Dinner with Drac" (1958) and "The Monster Mash" (1962) also fueled this hip new monster culture, as did plastic monster model kits, games, trading cards, and other assorted monster-abilia. Magazines devoted to classic and contemporary horror films proliferated, the most famous and enduring being *Famous Monsters of Filmland,* edited by jovial punster and monster movie überfan Forrest J. Ackerman. What all of this suggests is that when *Dark Shadows* went on the air in 1966, there was already a youthful fan base ready to respond to it—a fan base perhaps more interested in a humorous metatextual approach to the gothic genre than straightforward romance and suspense.

It is impossible to historicize *Dark Shadows* (or its ongoing fandom) without taking into account the show's camp appeal. Camp might best be described as a negotiated reading practice that ironically calls into question certain aspects of mainstream taste and especially how those aspects of taste relate to issues of gender and sexuality. During the first half of the twentieth century, a sort of "cult of camp" coalesced among urban gay men (and some women) in Western nations, specifically in relation to the era's dominant cultural/art form, Hollywood cinema. This cult laughed at the excesses of Hollywood's naive heterosexual melodramas, while simultaneously celebrating the indefatigable drive and bigger-than-life personas of actresses such as Joan Crawford, Bette Davis, Mae West, Barbara Stanwyck, Lana Turner, and Judy Garland. (One might easily add Joan Bennett to this list.) Camp aficionados also venerated "bad" actresses such as Maria Montez and "bad" (that is to say cheap or B) films, as well as the stylistic excesses of certain genres such as the musical, the melodrama, and the horror film. Seminal camp theorist Susan Sontag even went so far as to suggest that "the origins of camp taste are to be found [in] Gothic novels" ("Notes," 109). Perhaps most importantly, "the camp sensibility is one that is alive to a double sense in which some things can be taken . . . between the thing as meaning something, anything, and the thing as pure artifice" (ibid., 110). In other words, camp texts construct a subject position that is at least dual, if not multiple. In the case of *Dark Shadows* and its reception, the pleasures of the text may arise from its straightforward narrative and character development, although its pleasures can also be more complex, based on a simultaneously ironic reading of the text that undermines or queers its surface meanings. Just as the actor/character complexes discussed in the previous chapter encouraged a metatextual response to the show, so too did its overall tone, as actors struggled to maintain straight faces while stumbling through their lines or accidentally knocking over Styrofoam tombstones.

By the mid-1960s, the camp sensibility was becoming increasingly mainstreamed. Susan Sontag's "Notes on Camp" (first published in 1964 and anthologized in 1966) is a good indicator of how the homosexual cult of camp was being absorbed into multiple arenas of popular culture production and reception. Although Sontag downplayed the queerer origins of camp taste and aesthetics, she did take care to differentiate between what she called naive camp and deliberate camp (110–12). Naive camp is the form of camp that is closest to its queer origins and is created through the process of reception: savvy audiences decode "serious" texts as humorous because of their bad acting, low production values, and/or cliché-ridden dialogue. Deliberate camp is created by a text's producers, who purposefully encode "bad" production values into their texts. More recent theorists of camp also distinguish between queer camp—dedicated to destabilizing normative genders and sexualities—and its more mainstream appropriation pop camp—verging on mere parody with less deconstruction of normative values (Meyer, *Politics*, 1–22). Thus, while the work of 1960s experimental filmmakers such as Kenneth Anger, Jack Smith, Andy Warhol, and John Waters should all be considered deliberate queer camp—because they knowingly critique or interrogate Hollywood style as well as cultural assumptions about gender and sexuality—it was more mainstream pop camp that became the flavor of the day in television shows like *Batman, Lost in Space* (CBS, 1965–68), and *The Wild Wild West* (CBS, 1965–69). At the movies, horror and science fiction films like *Frankenstein Created Woman* (1967), *Barbarella* (1968), *Dr. Jekyll and Sister Hyde* (1971), *Lust for a Vampire* (1971), and *The Abominable Dr. Phibes* (1971) also flirted with more or less deliberate and queer camp sensibilities.

As is hopefully apparent by now, *Dark Shadows* creates countless opportunities to be appreciated as naive camp, what Sontag described as the camp of "seriousness that fails" ("Notes," 112). From its generic story lines, full-throttle performances, cheap sets, and outlandish narrative events, *Dark Shadows* almost begs to be decoded as camp: what is meant to be frightening is also often ludicrously amusing. Speaking of those issues in retrospect, many of the show's creators recognized that they were creating camp. Director John Sedwick, for example, drew a distinction between *Dark Shadows*' naive camp style by contrasting it with the era's best-known example of deliberate camp, saying, "We could not camp it up. It had to be treated like he [Barnabas] was a real vampire living in a real mansion like Collinwood . . . without the POWS! and ZAPS! like *Batman* did" (quoted in Scott, *Companion*, 121). Actress Lara Parker attributes much of the show's camp effect to its actors. "Many of the performances—Jonathan [Frid]'s, Grayson [Hall]'s, Thayer [David]'s, Humbert [Allen Astredo]'s, Louis [Edmonds]'—to name just a few, were larger than life. Most of us were stage actors, not soap opera actors. We were trained to make the emotions broad and powerful, rather than internalized and underplayed" (quoted in ibid., 16). Addressing naive camp directly, Parker continues: "[We] never played these scenes for laughs. If *Dark Shadows* was ever 'camp,' as some have said, it was not because we thought it was funny, or ever took it less than seriously. The more incredible the story was, the more fervently and passionately we portrayed it" (ibid., 17).

Yet there is often a thin line between naive and deliberate camp. We may never know to what degree some of the performers may have deliberately camped up their roles, although it is not hard to see actors like Christopher Pennock and Thayer David metaphorically winking underneath their wigs and false mustaches. (Allegedly, Pennock would occasionally tape his scenes after ingesting hallucinogenic drugs, suggesting his aim to treat the show in a more deliberately mocking manner.) And surely the series' writers must have amused themselves by trying

75

An I-Ching experiment goes terribly wrong for a day player, resulting in her spectacular demise, a typical gothic shock effect that is simultaneously horrifying and hilarious.

to outdo the outlandishness of previous episodes. But whether naive or deliberate, pop or queer, *Dark Shadows'* camp appeal is one of its strongest drawing points, one that many fans of the show appreciated immediately, while others "grew into it" as they got older. Many fans who were children when they first watched the show recall that they originally responded to it in a more straightforward sense—taking its gothic chills at face value—even as they later developed a more complex reading protocol. As one such fan put it, "Now I appreciate the show's campiness and (strangely at the same time) the emotional depth and pathos of some of its characters and stories" (quoted in Benshoff, "Resurrection," 53). This is the essence of *Dark Shadows'* camp appeal—it allows the viewer to appreciate the thrills and chills of its diegetic gothic narrative, while simultaneously allowing him or her to be an affectionately acerbic critic totally outside the text.

The rest of this chapter examines some of the ways that *Dark Shadows* was discussed in the popular press during its initial run and explores the multiple ways that it was marketed via its secondary texts. In these respects, *Dark Shadows* again seems to predate certain developments within more recent soap operas. For example, the following comments made by historian Robert C. Allen about "normal" soap operas (circa the mid-1980s) also describe the function and appeal of *Dark Shadows* (a text his seminal study *Speaking of Soap Operas* never mentions). As Allen puts it, the "perspectival openness of the contemporary soap opera diegesis enables it to accommodate a far greater range of 'negotiated' readings than other, more normatively determinant forms of fictive narratives. Furthermore, this openness helps to account for the broadening of the soap opera audience in recent years to include more men, adolescents, and college students" (174). Indeed, *Dark Shadows* did appeal to a wide variety of audiences—including men as well as women, children and adolescents, conservatives and hippies. Although *Dark Shadows* was initially received by the press as traditional

Christopher Pennock, seen here as Leviathan man-beast Jeb Hawkes, played all of his roles to the hilt, allegedly even occasionally acting under the influence of psychoactive drugs.

gothic romance, it was soon being discussed in terms of its camp and countercultural appeals. As such, for some commentators the show moved from being harmless escapism to something far more sinister—a show that potentially encouraged drug use and other antisocial behaviors.

Dark Shadows was occasionally mentioned in the popular press during its pre-Barnabas months, but seemingly to little point or effect. *TV Guide* ran its first article on the show in its December 3, 1966, issue. Titled "Giddy Gothic," the short photo-essay focuses primarily on the show's sets: comparing and contrasting the exteriors of Collinwood (actual locations in upstate New York) with the studio sets in Manhattan. There is little mention of any element that would become central to the show's ongoing appeal, except for the trickery of the production process. By the summer of 1967, however, after the introduction of Barnabas, *Dark Shadows* began to get much more media attention. A full-page article on the show and its newfound popularity appeared in the July 30, 1967, edition of the *New York Times*. In it, author Joan Barthel interviews Dan Curtis, Joan Bennett, and Jonathan Frid and specifically compares *Dark Shadows* to "latter day Hitchcock." The essay tries to account for the show's popularity in terms of gothic romanticism—as opposed to overt sexuality—suggesting that "it may be that the ladies out there in detergent land are at the edge of their ennui with all the erotic goings-on in the standard soap. Alienated from adultery. Bored with the bedroom" ("Detergent Land"). Yet, despite this attempted disclaimer, a sizable portion of the article discusses how women were responding to the show in a *very* sexualized manner and in particular to Barnabas Collins as played by Jonathan Frid. It reports that Frid was receiving over three hundred fan letters a week, many from women offering themselves to him. One such letter is excerpted and quoted: "I wish he'd bite me in the neck. I get so excited, I could smoke a whole pack of cigarettes just watching him." Other women reportedly sent nude pictures of themselves to the vampire star.

These comments attest to the fact that *Dark Shadows* did (and does) deliver an erotic thrill along with its supernatural shudders, following the usual patterns of repression displacement that so often characterize the gothic/horror genre. Thus, while many viewers did relate to *Dark Shadows* in an erotic way, apparently finding its sexual frissons to be its main appeal, other viewers could champion the show for its alleged exact opposite: its difference from "all the other [soap operas] during the day, with all the sex, abortions and illegal pregnancies" (quoted in Barthel, "Detergent Land"). Comments like these suggest interesting things about the reception of gothic texts. If one situates the gothic form within the larger Western Christian (or American Puritan) tradition of sexual repression, it is not hard to imagine the psychic mechanisms at work within the minds of the gothic's naive readers. By displacing the topics of sex and sexuality onto monstrous signifiers, the gothic invites its readers to experience the thrill of the sexually deviant within the safe or "innocent" zone of a fictional, make-believe generic construct. As the recent book *Queer Gothic* suggests, gothic "terror is almost always a sexual terror, and fear, and flight, and incarceration, and escape are almost always colored by the exoticism of transgressive sexual aggression" (Haggerty, 2). The author concludes that the entire genre of gothic literature—much of it written before the naming and "invention" of heterosexuality and homosexuality in the late 1800s—actually comprises its own complex and systemic model of human sexuality, one quite different from and much more varied than contemporary models would have us believe. Thus, whereas sophisticated readers may understand the gothic as about little else but sex, many of its consumers value it precisely for its manifest denial and/or repression of sexual content. (This dynamic appears to be at work once again in the recent Mormon-inflected "family values" vampires of Stephenie Meyer's *Twilight* books and films [2008, 2009, 2010].)

While the *New York Times* story was mostly complimentary and thoughtful, treating the show with some measure of respect—perhaps surprisingly given the soap opera's "low" cultural status—a short piece that appeared in *Newsweek* in August 1967 was far more snide, characterizing *Dark Shadows'* audience as "6.5 million housewives and shut-ins" ("The Ghoul Show," 60). Rather than compare the show to Hitchcock, *Newsweek* suggested it was Jonathan Frid's "campy élan" that was at the center of the show's appeal. Hinting at the sexual/nonsexual nature of his character, the essay suggests that Barnabas is "more Freudian than fiendish," but does not develop the idea beyond that brief assertion. These battles over the text's meaning(s)—was it high or low art? Sexual or not? Serious or silly?—would continue throughout the show's run and into its ongoing fandoms.

Many of these same fractures of meaning can be found in a *TV Guide* profile of Joan Bennett that appeared just a few days after the *Newsweek* article. The essay situates Joan Bennett firmly within a high art/low art dichotomy, depicting the aging star as a "refugee from the 'Great Era' [of Hollywood filmmaking] accepting her exile and professional demotion gracefully" (Efron, "No Tears," 12). As such, the essay hegemonically works to reinscribe old Hollywood as the glamorous dream factory that has become supplanted by trashy television, a decline both Bennett and the essay itself link almost directly to the rise of the counterculture. First Bennett nostalgically reminisces over the good old days: the "Golden Age is gone. . . . Almost all the people with great taste are gone—it was glamorous and fun and exciting." Then she attacks contemporary Hollywood as "an awfully funny group" of people making "filthy films" and decries the younger generations and what they were beginning to represent: "I can't bear the hippies and the beats. I think they're ghastly—they're not *clean.* Why are boys looking like girls and girls like boys? All this LSD business and the trips—it's awful." Intriguingly, Bennett finds this distressing unclean gender-bending to be at the heart of the counterculture but fails to see it as the repressed core of gothic horror in general. In fact, strong women (Angelique, Dr. Hoffman, Bennett's own character Elizabeth Collins Stoddard) and weak and/or hysterical men (Roger, Barnabas, Willie, and Quentin) were central to *Dark Shadows*' ongoing appeal. Furthermore, mods and hippies would populate the latter half of the series and become increasingly important to marketing the show. Bennett's own insecurities are perhaps best displayed by her comments about fellow Hollywood stars Bette Davis and Joan Crawford. Bennett feels their "grotesque roles" (in gothic horror films like *What Ever Happened to Baby Jane?* [1962], *Straight-Jacket* [1964], and *The Nanny* [1965]) have spoiled their glamorous Hollywood images, a tragic fate Bennett apparently feels she has escaped despite appearing on *Dark Shadows.*

By the summer of 1968, Jonathan Frid was receiving over two thousand fan letters a week, and the *Saturday Evening Post* reported that *Dark Shadows* was now "the top rated daytime attraction with females between the ages of 12 and 34" (Fox, "Vampire," 41). Numerous articles profiling Frid continued to appear in *TV Guide, Time, Newsweek,* the *Saturday Evening Post,* and any number of teen-oriented magazines such as *16 Magazine* and *Flip.* Most of them stress the tremendous fan response to Barnabas Collins, vampire, among both women and children. For example, *Time* magazine reported the show was then drawing "15 million viewers a week" and that at "a Fort Wayne shopping center, played by both Richard Nixon and Eugene McCarthy during the Indiana primary, Frid outdrew each of them—or so claims his press agent" ("Ship of Ghouls"). In the *Saturday Evening Post,* Frid himself was quoted on the surprising cultural response to his character: "I suppose women see Barnabas as a romantic figure because I play him as a lonely, tormented man rather than a Bela Lugosi villain" (quoted in Fox, "Vampire," 41). By this time Barnabas's backstory and tragic love affair with Josette DuPres had already been explored on the air; the show's rebranding of Barnabas from vicious monster to tragic gothic hero had apparently been immensely successful.

Although *Dark Shadows* was becoming enormously popular, it was also bucking a trend in daily soap operas that critics were then starting to notice. According to a *Newsweek* article from December 1968, soap operas in general were becoming more topical, even as there were significant limits to this new realism. As the essay put it, although "taboos are toppling faster than ratings are rising, a few cling like marine deck stain. Religion, homosexuality, and Vietnam are never discussed" (Waters, "New Sins," 104). In fact, *Dark Shadows* was taking on religion, if in an oblique way, through the witch-hunting character of Reverend Trask. Because the show more or less "sides" with its monsters and other gothic heroes, Trask is one of the few characters on the show who is truly and unrepentantly evil. A few fundamentalist Christians of the era did read *Dark Shadows* as an attack on traditional religion, and they circulated an editorial pamphlet that depicted the Devil watching *Dark Shadows* with the caption "Satan's Favorite TV Show" (Scott, *Companion*, 127). The same pamphlet was also used to protest *Bewitched*. Although *Dark Shadows* did altogether avoid any overt discussion of homosexuality or Vietnam, another ABC soap opera, *All My Children*, featured a Vietnam War protest story line when it premiered just two years later. It would take several more decades for the soaps to integrate openly homosexual characters with any degree of success.

In the late 1960s, however, the afternoon soaps were beginning to address broader aspects of the counterculture, including drugs, civil rights, and youthful rebellion. *Another World* featured an LSD-spiked cocktail, *One Life to Live* dramatized an interracial affair, and *Secret Storm* tackled student unrest at a large urban university (Waters, "New Sins," 100). Addressing race/racism on the soaps directly, the 1968 *Newsweek* article continued: "The integration of the sudsers may not seem especially startling in light of the racial advances currently being made throughout television. But in Soapland, where viewers have lived and intensely identified with a set of characters for several years, the introduction of the black face is a much trickier proposition. For example, when *Secret Storm* inserted a Negro singer last summer, the show was inundated with what one *Storm* writer calls an 'unbelievable' flood of hate mail" (ibid.).

As with sexuality, *Dark Shadows* neatly sidestepped both drugs and civil rights via its usual method of gothic displacement. Thus, although no one at Collinwood ever took recreational drugs, hallucinogenic experiences caused by spells and dreams occurred frequently; similarly, vampires and witches served as metaphoric Others rather than actual racial ones. In fact, aside from a few token African American and Asian American day players—most of whom never had any speaking lines—the world of *Dark Shadows* was a resolutely white place.

By 1969, the year of its highest ratings, *Dark Shadows* was ABC's most popular soap opera and was being watched by over twenty million viewers daily. This was the year that David Selby joined the cast as Quentin Collins, and he immediately began to rival Barnabas in popularity. Early in the year, *TV Guide*'s in-house reviewer Cleveland Amory wrote a bitchy review that slammed the show but also pegged its camp appeal, although he never used the word "camp" itself. Amory prefaced his remarks by stating that he would never have watched the show had he not been home in bed sick with the flu. He continued (and note the use of the royal we): "At the end of the week, by which time we had decided that the series was, in our considered judgment, the worst in the history of entertainment, we found that when Saturday came and there was no show, we missed it" (6). Despite the essay's rather flippant tone ("Take the actors—please!"), Amory ultimately arrives at "a true understanding of *Dark Shadows*' success—the worse it is, the more you'll love it." This appeal of the show's "badness" was a key component of *Dark Shadows*' naive camp aesthetic—and a reading of the show now officially sanctioned by *TV Guide*.

Actress Kathryn Leigh Scott (Maggie Evans, Josette DuPres) was the focus of another *TV Guide* profile in May 1969. The essay (written by a man) demonstrates an awkward and sometimes hostile negotiation of female independence and agency. At first, Scott's roles on the show are somewhat denigrated and infantilized as the article characterizes Maggie Evans as "the Jinxed Jane of ironing-board TV," a "Super Victim" of daytime television who is "always running around screaming 'Run! Run! Here come the ghoulies!'" (Higgins, "More Perils," 16). Then the essay taps into basic ideological assertions about the American dream, representing Scott as a poor but hardworking farm girl from Minnesota, whose recently immigrated family had been active in the Norwegian resistance movement during World War II. The essay then confronts her "independence" directly, even as it snidely links it to her alleged egotism and unwillingness to stand up for actual causes. "Miss Scott enjoys talking about herself and she's not a bit shy about mentioning her many good qualities and attitudes. . . . She opposes the war in Vietnam and resents 'paying taxes to support it.' Civil rights has her all in a lather. Yet she won't join picket lines. 'I'm too independent'" (ibid., 17). Curiously, the article goes on to quote two other actors who allude to Scott's egotism and insecurity, one of whom calls her "a bargain basement Saint Joan." Bitchy and gossipy, the article is a good example of the era's (male) discourses about the allegedly trivial nature of soap operas, the women who star in them, and the women who watch them.

In actuality, *Dark Shadows* was aimed at and marketed heavily to children and young adults of both sexes as well as housewives. Unlike *TV Guide* or *Newsweek,* the teen magazines of the era demonstrate how *Dark Shadows* was sold to younger audiences. Perhaps unsurprisingly, when compared to the "adult" press, there is a great deal of focus on the show's two child stars, David Henesy and Denise Nickerson. A *16 Magazine* from June 1969 also suggests the intensity of the *Dark Shadows* phenomenon: out of the magazine's sixty-eight pages, including the front and back cover, *Dark Shadows* is mentioned on at least fifteen of them, and two regular columns are devoted entirely to the show. Photographic portraits of the show's charismatic male monster stars—Jonathan Frid, David Selby, and Don Briscoe (who played both a werewolf and a vampire at varying points of the series)—package and present the actors as desirable hunks. Similarly, short features allegedly written by the actors describe their "hates and loves," presumably so the reader could tell if she and her favorite male *Dark Shadows* star would make a good romantic match. The actors are designated as "fave raves" and featured alongside color photos of much younger pop music stars like Bobby Sherman, Sajid, Enzo Cerusico, and John Cowsill. Aside from Denise Nickerson, no other female cast members are featured in this issue, which along with the male pinups suggests that the magazine itself was aimed squarely at girls and young women beginning to experience and express their sexuality. The same appeal obviously also targeted gay men, although that demographic could not be openly acknowledged within the pages of the magazine at that time.

By 1969, *Dark Shadows* was becoming something of a marketing juggernaut, with a huge range of secondary texts available for purchase. While such "branding" has become a key aspect of modern film and television cultures, *Dark Shadows'* extensive merchandising of ancillary themed products predates the contemporary boom by several decades. (Other nascent sci-fi/fantasy franchises of the era included *Batman* and *Planet of the Apes* [1968].) Among the most culturally prevalent of the *Dark Shadows* spin-off products was a series of thirty-two pulp novels written by Dan Ross but published under the female pseudonym Marilyn Ross. The first *Dark Shadows* novel had been published in 1966 and the last—*Barnabas, Quentin, and the Vampire Beauty*—was published in 1972, almost a year after the show was canceled. Usually centered on a young ingenue exploring the mysteries and romances of Collinwood, the novels made little attempt to integrate themselves with the television show's ongoing story lines, in effect creating their own Parallel Time and historical flashback narratives. Patterned as they were after the era's Harlequin romances, the novels seem squarely aimed at female readers of various ages. However, some latter-day male fans admit to first discovering *Dark Shadows* not via the TV screen, but instead via these novels. As one such reader relates, "I think it's a testament to the level of pop culture status that the show achieved that I became obsessed with it through spinoff merchandise" (Lamberson, "Remembering *Dark Shadows*"). Other *Dark Shadows* books published during its initial run include *Barnabas Collins: A Personal Picture Album* by Jonathan Frid (1969) and *The "Dark Shadows" Cookbook* (1970).

While men and boys could and did read *Dark Shadows* romances and flip through the pages of *16 Magazine*, there were other *Dark Shadows* secondary texts that seem to be aimed at

85

52·608 A Paperback Library Gothic 50¢

GOLD EDITION

A new novel of suspense
based on ABC-TV's

DARK SHADOWS
—daytime TV's most
popular series!

The Curse of Collinwood

Suddenly Victoria's life is threatened—by a man
who was murdered over 100 years ago!

Marilyn Ross

Over thirty *Dark Shadows* novels written by Marilyn (Dan) Ross were
marketed during and after the run of the show, most focusing on familiar characters in new or alternate narratives.

them more directly. *Barnabas Collins in a Funny Vein* (a book of sophomoric vampire jokes) and *The "Dark Shadows" Book of Vampires and Werewolves* are centered on humor and horror, respectively, and not gothic romance. The Gold Key/Whitman *Dark Shadows* comic books (1968–76) also seem more squarely aimed at male readers, their chief appeal being horror rather than romance. For example, in *Terror Flies by Night* (November 1970) Barnabas is drawn as a green-skinned ghoul locked in a battle of vengeance with Angelique. Heterosexual romance in this comic is relegated to a generic victim and her boyfriend, and its vampire attacks are more monstrous than seductive, accompanied by comic book shrieks rather than longing sighs. Boys as well as girls also bought and played with the plethora of *Dark Shadows* toys that were marketed during the era: chewing gum cards, Quentin Collins postcards, jigsaw puzzles, Magic Slates, Viewmaster 3-D reels, and board games all hit the market in 1969. They were soon followed by *Dark Shadows* costumes, masks, capes, fangs, rings, coloring books, wristwatches, and model kits.

The Barnabas Collins *Dark Shadows* Game from Milton Bradley was recommended for ages six to fourteen, and the box cover shows two boys and a girl playing with its "Glow-in-Dark" skeletons and "Set of Barnabas' 'fangs.'" While the ostensible object of the game was to assemble toy model skeletons part by part via a coded spinner, the inclusion of the fangs promised another way to enjoy the game. As the inside box lid reads, "The Toy Fangs are not part of the game and belong only to the owner of the game. They are placed over the teeth of a player to play the role of Barnabas Collins. (They should be washed before a player uses them.)" Here the chief appeal of *Dark Shadows* seems to be pretending to be a vampire, not being romantically involved with him. However, given the unpredictable nature of children's play, one can imagine all sorts of profligate possibilities afforded by a set of plastic Barnabas Collins fangs.

Perhaps the most obvious secondary text to circulate during

With their emphasis on monstrous attacks rather than romance, the Gold Key/Whitman *Dark Shadows* comic books were aimed at young male readers more so than women.

the show's run was its music. The album *Original Music from "Dark Shadows"* was released in 1969 and made it to number 18 on the Billboard record charts. "Quentin's Theme," recorded by the Charles Randolph Grean Sounde, also became a hit single, reaching number 13 on Billboard's "Hot 100 Singles" chart and number 3 on its "Easy Listening" chart (Scott and Pierson, *Almanac,* 147). While the Charles Randolph Grean Sounde single was an instrumental arrangement, "Quentin's Theme" on the *Dark Shadows* sound track features a voice-over by actor David Selby, emphasizing the music's romantic longing:

> Shadows of the night
> Falling silently
> Echo of the past
> Calling me to you.

In fact, the sound track album is mostly designed around implied romances with Barnabas and Quentin. In addition to the show's popular main title theme music, the album has six tracks of voice-overs by Jonathan Frid or David Selby meant to invoke tragic romanticism and sexual frissons, not cheap scares or monstrous attacks. For example, on the cut "I, Barnabas," Jonathan Frid intones that

> I, Barnabas, lie in deep sleep on my bed of purple velvet,
>   Asleep, but awake to your thoughts, your feelings, your desires.
>   Alone, but cradled by the presence of your mind, I hear your call.
>   I feel your yearning, I know that you want me, I know that you need me.

Of course, such literally "purple" prose and overweening romanticism also makes the entire album ripe for a camp reading. However, the album was packaged with a mini-poster featuring both actors in "normal" publicity shots as well as in full character makeup, suggesting again a target audience of women and adolescent girls.

By 1970, as the show's popularity cooled a bit, yet another *Dark Shadows* audience was suddenly discovered by the mainstream press: hippies and drug users. In the April 20 *Newsweek* essay "Turned-On Vampire," Jonathan Frid mulls over his appeal to countercultural audiences: "Youngsters today are looking for a new morality . . . and so is Barnabas. . . . Just like the kids today, he's confused—lost, screwed-up, and searching for something" (103). However, the essay also suggests something more sinister may be going on when it explains that *Dark Shadows* is not just mindless entertainment for children and addlepated housewives. It suggests (and note the drug lingo) that "many college students—and even a few professors—are also hooked on the *Dark Shadows* habit." Making the latent manifest, the essay continues: although "*Dark Shadows* is no longer quite as 'in' as it once was on campus—many students now dismiss the program as 'teeny bopper fantasy'—thousands of students still watch it fanatically, often after turning on with marijuana or drugs. On the University of Chicago campus, one student reports that 'I know five scag [heroin] freaks who watch it religiously. They shoot up in the afternoon to watch. The show's supernatural ugly vibes are just right for when you are strung out on scag.'" Although heroin-enhanced *Dark Shadows* viewing parties in the middle of the afternoon seem highly improbable—let alone heroin withdrawal viewing parties—the nature of the assertion seems to be part of the era's larger discursive project to rebrand the meaning of the counterculture from "peace and love" to "drugs and death." This complex hegemonic backlash was obviously precipitated by many factors, including the rise of President Richard M. Nixon's "law and order" platform as well as the highly publicized crimes committed by the Manson family in late 1969.

"Turned-On Vampire" even lends credence to the fundamentalist Christian argument that *Dark Shadows* was encouraging young people to practice the black arts, quoting one such "dabbler in the occult [who] believes many practitioners of witchcraft take the show seriously as 'a watered-down version of the real truth'" (103). While *Dark Shadows* had been silly trashy entertainment for women and children just a few months ago, it was now being linked to heroin, satanism, and even anarchy in the mainstream press. The show's aesthetics are now almost completely contained within either psychedelic discourses or as part of the campy "Cult of Bad"—no more allusions to Hitchcock. For example, *Rolling Stone* editor John Carroll is quoted describing the show as "incredibly bad. That's why it's so good. It has no redeeming social value." Like much of the counterculture itself, *Dark Shadows* was being defined as antithetical to dominant middle-class morality.

With its popularity waning, *Dark Shadows* was canceled by ABC in the spring of 1971. Nonetheless, the show still had many ardent admirers, many of whom would become (or already were) founding members of multiple and varied *Dark Shadows* fan clubs. A few weeks after the cancellation, one dedicated fan wrote to *TV Guide* to lament her loss. The letter is worth quoting in its entirety, for it sums up the way many *Dark Shadows* fans felt then (and continue to feel) about the show:

> Our television set is turned off this 4 p.m. in mourning for the passing of the most fabulously innovative program ever to have graced TV—*Dark Shadows,* that exquisitely mounted and star-adorned daily feast for the eyes. We are bereft. Why, in the name of imaginative beauty, are retarded soap operas with their litany of tears, infidelity, and unwanted pregnancies, permitted interminable pollution of the airwaves, while a production of lush charm and tension-relaxing imagery can be supplanted by—ye

gods!—yet another talk show? I am grateful to ABC for the beauty (some scenes were Rembrandts in motion), and the fantasy (a delightful way to unwind after battle with a prosaic world) and the inspired casting. *Password* indeed! (Feehan, letter to the editor, A2)

Dark Shadows, the original gothic television soap opera, may have ceased production, but its afterlife was just beginning.

Legacy

Dark Shadows' legacy has been long lasting, both among dedicated fans as well as professional media producers. In addition to the comic books, novels, and sound track music discussed previously, this chapter considers several other industrially produced texts directly related to Dark Shadows, including the two films based on the original show (featuring the same cast), and the 1991 prime-time remake (which used a completely different set of actors). This chapter also examines Dark Shadows' more subtle and pervasive effects on the changing nature of fantasy/horror entertainment and specifically the evolving representation of the vampire in popular culture. For while vampires before Dark Shadows tended to be mostly evil creatures in need of eradication, recent decades have seen the evolution of the "new vampire," a kinder, gentler, more humanized being in search of love and understanding (Zanger, "Metaphor to Metonymy"). Although it is hard to claim (let alone prove) that any single text has definitively changed the course of media history, Dark Shadows did play an important part in this discursive shift. Dark Shadows also needs to be seen as an important historical antecedent to today's popular gothic/fantasy franchises, especially since it was one of the first such franchises to realize both the narrative importance of serialization as well as the (now given) need to extend such a franchise across varying and multiple platforms (Grainge, *Brand Hollywood;* Jenkins, *Convergence Culture;* Mittell, "Narrative Complexity"; Newman, "Beats to Arcs").

Dark Shadows' influence on other fantasy and horror texts began even while it was still being aired on ABC. One of the more interesting of these artifacts was the syndicated soap opera *Strange Paradise* (1969–70), a show deliberately crafted on the *Dark Shadows* template. Set on a Caribbean island, but shot in Canada, *Strange Paradise* originally centered on a wealthy nobleman trying to use occult magic and voodoo rites to revive his dead wife. Although the series is very difficult to see today, clips of the show on YouTube reveal many similarities to *Dark Shadows,* from a central drawing room set with a grand staircase to a heavy focus on ancestral portraits, secret rooms, reincarnated identities, and various spells and curses. (This is perhaps unsurprising, since writer Ron Sproat and producer Robert Costello worked on both shows.) Several of the male characters are as shaggy and muttonchopped as Quentin Collins, and the end credit sequence—rolling over an empty set from that day's episode—is the same effect used on *Dark Shadows.* While some of *Strange Paradise's* fans remember it as being effectively frightening, the show could not compete with its progenitor (nor did it have network backing) and did not last long in the media marketplace.

More successful was *House of Dark Shadows,* the first feature film based on the soap opera, which became something of a hit in the fall of 1970. Written by series writers Sam Hall and Gordon Russell, it was produced and directed by Dan Curtis and starred most of the show's central cast. Receiving generally positive reviews, the GP-rated film was far more bloody and violent than the television show could be. It also compressed months of story line (from 1967 and 1968) into a ninety-seven-minute linear narrative following Barnabas as he is released from his coffin, wreaks havoc at Collinwood, lusts for Maggie/Josette, is briefly cured by Julia, and is eventually stalked, staked, and destroyed. Comparing the film with the television show reveals significant differences in narrative style. Unlike the soap opera, the film almost completely eschews paradigmatic character development in favor of syntagmatic action sequences; audiences were perhaps expected to attend the film with foreknowledge of Collinwood's complex character relations. (There is still a metatextual appeal to character and actor though, as the show's less central cast members appear in different minor roles in the film, creating a sort of "spot the cameo" game for viewers in the know.) More severe fates could also be meted out to the film version's characters—by the end of it, almost everyone in the cast is dead, including Barnabas but also Carolyn, Roger, Willie, Julia, and Professor Stokes.

95

Just as the soap opera was being increasingly discussed in the popular press as camp, so too was *House of Dark Shadows* advertised in a deliberately campy way, underscoring its multiple appeals as romance, horror, and humor. Comically playing up the vampire-romance angle, one tagline suggested that "Now there is a vampire film for the two of you." Another advertisement featured a two-shot of Barnabas and Maggie with the caption "A couple in love like any other couple except one is a vampire." Gimmicks and promotions for the film included vampire cocktails at theater concession stands and a Miss American Vampire contest. Perhaps most campy and queer, in the film's trailer a Boris Karloff impersonator tells potential audience members that "Barnabas Collins, vampire, takes a bride in a bizarre act of unnatural love," then salaciously invites viewers to "come and see how the vampires *do it!*" Whereas sex and sexuality (no matter how "normal" or bizarre)—and deliberate camp—were downplayed on the television show (and only slightly more obvious in the GP-rated film), they were nonetheless chief selling points of *House of Dark Shadows.*

Night of Dark Shadows appeared one year later, and was again (re)viewed through the lens of camp. As the *Los Angeles Times* opined, "If the earlier film was at times a slapdash affair, its campy horror was still fun. But deliberate camp is scarcely a novelty anymore, and this very careless-looking sequel is quickly silly and tiresome" (Thomas, "Familiar Look"). In truth, *Night of Dark Shadows* was not constructed as deliberate camp in the *Batman* vein; it is a relatively complex and moody reincarnation story that everyone plays straight (thus making its camp naive). Partly because so many characters were killed in the first film—and actor Frid was eager to move on—*Night* is about past sins and spiritual possession, not vampires. The story is only indirectly related to the original series and centers on Quentin Collins (David Selby), his new bride Tracy (Kate Jackson), and the lustful spirit of condemned witch Angelique (Lara Parker). The film might best be described as a sort of ghost story version of *Rebecca;* indeed, a reference to *Rebecca*'s surly housekeeper Mrs. Danvers is made in the film's opening moments. Just as she played that character when the original soap opera did its own version of *Rebecca,* Grayson Hall again brings her queer appeal to *Night*'s menacing housekeeper Carlotta Drake. It is Carlotta's "love" for Angelique that keeps her spirit "alive" and haunting the Great House. Together Carlotta and Angelique hope to see Quentin Collins fully possessed by his ancestor Charles Collins so that Angelique and Charles may continue to carry on their adulterous affair from centuries ago. As in the soap opera, Quentin Collins is rather a passive male acted on by supernatural forces rather than embodying them himself.

Night of Dark Shadows did not fare well with critics or with many fans—perhaps because it lacked the vampire Barnabas Collins. The film is also rather disjointed and confusing, partly due to the fact that it was hastily cut by its distributor MGM from 129 minutes to 97 minutes, allegedly just days and hours before its premiere. (In 1999, dedicated fan Darren Gross discovered the missing footage from the film, but not the sound track elements. As of this writing, there has been no completed restoration.) One of the more intriguing aspects of *Night* is its one-sheet poster, a complex graphic that exploits millennia-old fears of the *vagina dentata*. The poster incorporates four different representations of Angelique: the hanged witch Angelique and her white clad spirit are shown overlapping each other, while a third image (positioned over the legs of the hanged body) shows Angelique in an embrace with Charles/Quentin. However, positioned in the middle of the hanged body's torso is a close-up image of Angelique, her face rendered with a skeletal and bloody red maw positioned at the level of the full figure's pelvic girdle. The image readily suggests a monstrous and devouring toothed vagina, implying that Angelique's queer gothic sexuality encompasses both necrophilia as well as insatiable, potentially castrating female desire. (As one of the film's taglines put it, "Her return from the grave is just the beginning of their lust.") This shift in Angelique's character from empowered witchy-woman to monstrous sexual creature is perhaps another reason the film failed to speak to even its target audience. As does the poster, the film (at least as it presently exists) does not develop Angelique's backstory or character motivations (as did the television show), instead it seems more designed to play upon the era's male fears of strong, sexual women. In this way, *Night of Dark Shadows* seems more closely linked to the era's lesbian vampire films than to the gothic soap opera that gave rise to it.

When Dan Curtis brought *Dark Shadows* back to the small screen in 1991, he chose the original Barnabas narrative to be the show's central story line. Like the films, the prime-time remake of *Dark Shadows* features much better production values than the original soap opera, although the scale model of Collinwood that graces the title sequence is rather obvious. Since the original *Dark Shadows* cast was considered too old to reprise their roles, new actors were chosen. Handsome British

The *Night of Dark Shadows* one-sheet poster from 1971 suggests that Angelique possess a monstrous and devouring *vagina dentata*.

character actor Ben Cross was hired to play Barnabas, while in an inspired bit of casting, 1960s European horror film star Barbara Steele was hired to play Julia. Again, an aging Hollywood star—this time Jean Simmons—was hired to play Elizabeth Collins Stoddard, while younger actors of various backgrounds rounded out the cast. As in the original Barnabas story line, the revival series begins as Willie releases Barnabas from his coffin and includes historical sequences that explain his backstory. However, while the remake remains fairly faithful to its original source material, there were some interesting changes made, perhaps reflecting the bed-hopping nature of that era's primetime serials. (*Melrose Place* [Fox, 1992–99] would debut one year later.) Thus Roger Collins is no longer crypto-gay; instead he is a robust heterosexual having an affair with Maggie Evans, who herself dabbles in witchcraft. Because of this change, it is governess Victoria Winters who Barnabas imagines to be the reincarnation of his long-lost Josette. *Dark Shadows* fans were split over the show—many had hoped in vain for cameos from original cast members—but the remake was not renewed by NBC beyond its original twelve-episode commitment (see Pierson, *Resurrected* for an overview of the series).

Aside from the movies and the revival serial, the original *Dark Shadows* has also had effects on popular culture in more indirect ways. Dan Curtis did become something of a gothic auteur in the 1970s, bringing elements of his style (and by extension *Dark Shadows*' style) to a number of film and television texts. Curtis's 1972 television movie *The Night Stalker* also centers on a modern-day vampire; it was so successful it was spun off into the series *Kolchak: The Night Stalker* (ABC, 1974–75). (That series was remade by ABC in 2005 but lasted for only ten episodes.) However, due to its series and not serial nature, *Kolchak* quickly devolved into a "monster of the week" formula, with Darren McGavin's crusty reporter Carl Kolchak investigating a different supernatural event each week. Without the ongoing character development afforded by serial form, horror television (like horror cinema) more readily treats its heroes and monsters as Manichean opposites and not complex characters. The importance of serial form to long-lasting and complex horror/fantasy texts was (re)discovered by network producers in the 1990s, when shows like *The X-Files* (Fox, 1993–2002) and *Buffy the Vampire Slayer* (WB, UPN, 1997–2003) took great pains to develop ongoing story arcs in addition to their "monster of the week" episodic structures.

Perhaps most importantly, *Dark Shadows* was part of an important discursive trend in recent decades toward softening the image of the vampire from a bloodthirsty antagonist into a romantic protagonist. Originally, Count Dracula as envisioned in Bram Stoker's 1897 novel was quite a monster, feeding human babies to his vampire brides. The first cinematic vampire, Graf Orlok (Max Schreck) in F. W. Murnau's *Nosferatu* (1922) was a ratlike predator, not a romantic leading man. Bela Lugosi does exhibit a softer, seductive side to the vampire in the classical Hollywood film *Dracula* (1931)—contemporary audiences may forget that his performance is suggestive of that era's Latin-lover stereotype—but he nonetheless is still an unnatural thing that must be vanquished. Similarly, when *Dark Shadows* first went on the air, the most iconic cinematic vampire was Christopher Lee as Count Dracula in numerous Hammer films, and he was far from romantic. Rather than slip gracefully into maidens' hearts and bedchambers with seductive charms, Lee's Dracula was more likely to throw open their bedroom doors and rip into their throats with savage violence. The fact that Lee's Dracula hardly has any dialogue in some of these films also suggests he was meant to be understood as a vile and unstoppable creature and not a tragic romantic figure as Barnabas Collins eventually became.

In his essay "From Metaphor to Metonymy," Jules Zanger identifies this kinder, gentler creature as the "new vampire." As part of a general trend in films of recent decades that contain "sympathetic figures of social and psychic *otherness* at the repressed core of alien monstrosity" (Guerrero, *Framing Blackness*, 68), Zanger argues that images of vampires in recent decades have shifted "from solitary to multiple and communal, from metaphoric Anti-Christ to secular sinner, [and] from magical to mundane" ("Metaphor to Metonymy," 19). Exemplifying this trend, Zanger cites Anne Rice's *Vampire Chronicles* and the films based on them, the television show *Forever Knight* (CBS, 1992–96) about a vampire police detective, and Fred Saberhagen's vampire novels wherein "Dracula is the benevolent protector of his human friends" (ibid.). All of these traits are evident in the original *Dark Shadows* soap opera, as is the more modern idea that vampirism is a blood disease that might be cured by contemporary science. One of the most important ways *Dark Shadows* softened the vampire into a romantic protagonist was via the Josette-reincarnated-as-Maggie story line. Although this trope dates back at least to Universal's *The Mummy* (1932)—wherein Boris Karloff's immortal Im-Ho-Tep finds his lost lover Princess Anck-es-en-Amon reincarnated in the form of a contemporary socialite, *Dark Shadows* marks one of the first times that the trope was incorporated into a vampire story. It was quickly copied by other vampire films of the era, such as the blaxploitation horror film *Blacula* (1972). Today, it has almost become a standard aspect of the Dracula myth thanks to Francis Ford Coppola's *Bram Stoker's Dracula* (1992), which despite its title, added a reincarnated lover backstory between Count Dracula and Mina Harker that is nowhere present in Stoker's novel.

101

Although bloodthirsty and monstrous vampires continue to appear in film and television, they are just as likely to be reconfigured as heroic figures (as in the Joss Whedon shows *Buffy the Vampire Slayer* and *Angel* [WB, 1999–2004]) or as more obvious metaphorical figures based on actual social differences. For example, the HBO series *True Blood* (2008–), based on a series of novels by Charlaine Harris, creates a direct analogy between vampires and the evolving understanding of gay rights.

Within the narrative, a synthetic blood product has been invented so that vampires can choose to "come out of the coffin" and assimilate into mainstream society. However, rednecks and evangelicals persist in persecuting them. A church sign during the opening credits that reads "God Hates Fangs" is a quite deliberate pun on the "God Hates Fags" rhetoric spewed by some fundamentalist preachers. Like many if not most of these "new vampire" texts, *True Blood* is a serial narrative that centers on a reluctant vampire (Bill Compton played by Stephen Moyer) and his romance with a human female (Sookie Stackhouse played by Anna Paquin). While there are people who oppose the vampire protagonist, it is clear that Bill and Sookie's heterosexual romance is at the heart of the show's appeal, despite his being a vampire. Also like *Dark Shadows*, *True Blood* has explored Bill's origins with historical flashbacks, and its setting—the small Louisiana town of Bon Temps—is as crowded with supernatural Others as Collinsport ever was, including shape-shifters, werewolves, a potential witch, and a multitude of other vampires far less interested in mainstreaming than Bill.

Since the 1970s, the genres of horror, fantasy, and science fiction (and often hybrid combinations of two or more of them) have become driving forces in contemporary media culture. Whereas once these genres were ghettoized as B movie fodder for immature adults and precocious children, today they are central to the very formula of mainstream blockbuster franchising. Their fantastic spaces invite audiences into imaginative worlds and allow for the metaphoric exploration of actual human differences, even as that trend potentially recloses human differences behind monstrous signifiers. For example, it has been noted that Peter Jackson's Middle Earth in his *Lord of the Rings* trilogy (2001–3) contains no black characters—only black-coded monsters. *Avatar* (2009) uses the color blue to signify its racial Others, barely disguising the fact that they are meant to suggest Native Americans caught up in the white Western world's genocidal imperialism. Similarly, gay people in the *Harry Potter* universe are mostly metaphorized as bachelor wizards or werewolf schoolteachers. (The uproar that author J. K. Rowling created by "outing" the wizard Dumbledore demonstrates that many audiences actively seek to deny such readings.) It seems that contemporary Hollywood prefers metaphoric antagonists to real-life ones, since monsters and wizards (unlike real-life minorities) do not have antidefamation leagues. Thus a science fiction western like *Serenity* (2005) can feature stereotypical bloodthirsty Indians, as long as they are refigured as cannibalistic monsters from outer space called "Reavers."

Dark Shadows certainly did not invent gothic horror or fantasy—but it did reconfigure gothic literature and horror cinema into serial narratives for a media-savvy generation. In so doing, *Dark Shadows* prefigured today's blockbuster media franchises, not just textually or diegetically, but also industrially. The multiple platforms that *Dark Shadows* was presented on foreshadows contemporary Hollywood's synergistic practices. Far from being meaningless fluff, fantasy franchises like *Dark Shadows, Harry Potter, Twilight,* and *The Lord of the Rings* penetrate deep into Western cultures and continue to contribute to the ongoing hegemonic negotiation of real-world issues and ideologies.

Chapter 8

Fans and Fandom

Since at least the 1970s, media scholars have used ethno- **105** graphic research to study the ways that actual audience members make sense of televisual texts, especially soap operas. Following on the ideas and formulations of early cultural studies researchers such as Stuart Hall, David Morley, and Dorothy Hobson (see *Culture Media Language*), Ien Ang studied the reception of *Dallas* (CBS, 1978–91) among women in the Netherlands (*Watching "Dallas"*). Ellen Seiter, H. Borchers, G. Kreutzner, and E. Warth (*Remote Control*); Mary Ellen Brown (*Women's Culture; Women's Talk*); and Christine Geraghty (*Women and Soap*) have all explored the complex and often contradictory roles that various soap operas play in women's lives. In more recent years, Robert Allen and many others have increasingly explored the ways that soap operas "make sense" within national, international, and diasporic contexts (Allen, *To Be Continued;* Gillespie, *Television;* Katz and Liebes, "Mutual Aid"; Miller, "*Young and the Restless*"). Still other scholars have used ethnographic tools to investigate science fiction and fantasy fandoms (Jenkins, *Textual Poachers;* Tulloch and Jenkins, *Science Fiction*), arguing that their special generic positioning situates them especially well for the creation of multiple and diverse fandoms. In some cases, tertiary fan productions reread and rewrite the primary text in surprising ways, a fact that has led some cultural critics to champion fan cultures' potential for subverting the ideological status quo. As this chapter explores, such instances of subversion can be found within *Dark Shadows* fan culture, even as other fans continue to enjoy the show and (re)write it more in accordance with dominant ideologies. In other words, the primary text's dual appeal—straightforward gothic horror and the campy reappropriation thereof—also structures much of *Dark Shadows*' fandom.

Currently, *Dark Shadows* exists as an ever-increasing multi-tude of texts produced both "legitimately" by certain sectors of the media industry as well as by the fans themselves. Like their science fiction brethren, *Dark Shadows* fans attend conventions, lobby television producers, write and publish fanzines (now mostly replaced by websites), and/or produce other artifacts based on the show such as amateur theatricals and video tapes. YouTube is awash in homemade *Dark Shadows* videos, includ-ing music videos that reedit episodes to the beat of suggestive songs, clips that reenact favorite scenes with action figure dolls, serious tributes to favorite actors/characters, and actual footage of *Dark Shadows* stars speaking at various public appearances. Most of these fan productions are grounded in a love for and devotion to the show; they are not officially sanctioned by the show's producers nor created for anyone's profit. Some even come with disclaimers to that effect: "The authors know they do not own these wonderful men and women. . . . There is no $$$$ exchanged here, just a common love for the people who populate the *Dark Shadows* universe" (www.squidge.org). That said, such disclaimers do not always stop corporate law-yers—often from the music industry—from disabling websites because of copyright infringement.

Like the varied artifacts they produce, *Dark Shadows* fans come in all shapes and sizes, ages, races, ethnicities, classes, genders, abilities, and sexualities. Critical essays about *Dark*

Shadows' fan cultures began appearing in the 1990s and were based on open-ended surveys, fan interviews (both formal and informal), fan correspondence, and participation and observation at several national *Dark Shadows* conventions (Benshoff, "Resurrection"; "Secrets"). Those essays also assessed fanzines, video tapes, and other material artifacts from the first twenty years or so of *Dark Shadows* fan production. Returning to this research in the twenty-first century, one can see how drastically all media fan cultures have been reshaped due to the rise of the Internet and its ever-easier modes of web-based publishing and communication. *Dark Shadows* fans' productions may have begun with mimeographed fanzines and crude pencil drawings, but they have evolved into extensive web-based forums, complete with specialized chat rooms, listservs, and even an online encyclopedia, the CollinWiki, "A collaborative project designed to document everything related to the various incarnations of the *Dark Shadows* franchise." As of May 2009, the CollinWiki contained over 1,400 articles, a number its founders suggest is just "the tip of the iceberg" since "the site is still in its infancy" (http://darkshadows.wikia.com/wiki/Dark_Shadows). Other recent developments include online role-playing games and the creation of *machinima* shorts, as fans use video game software to create their own original *Dark Shadows* episodes (see *Dark Shadows the Werewolf Connection* on YouTube).

Dark Shadows fan clubs began during the original run of the series, although much of that initial wave of activity (contests, promotional events, etc.) was actively orchestrated by the show's producers. Other fans organized in groups on an ad hoc basis. Some, like the Fanatic Followers of Frid (a.k.a. the 3-F Society), devoted themselves solely to the vampire star, while others—like those in the New York area who held vigils outside the show's Manhattan studio—hoped to meet and greet anyone associated with the show. One such fan, Jay Nass, has posted his home movie footage of those events on YouTube as part of the short film *Dark Shadows: A Fan Remembers*. According to the

"Dark Shadows" Almanac, the first *Dark Shadows* fan convention occurred in 1977 and was "actually just a small get-together at a general science fiction convention, Starcon, in San Diego, California. Two years later, in 1979, the first convention expressly for *Dark Shadows* was held—ShadowCon, became an annual event in Los Angeles through 1985" (Scott and Pierson, 207). The competing *Dark Shadows* Festival began in 1983 in New York, coinciding with the reappearance of *Dark Shadows* on local PBS stations throughout that area. Although there have been other more sporadic and specific *Dark Shadows* conventions throughout the years, the annual *Dark Shadows* Festival continues to be the primary place for fans to gather in person and to meet the show's surviving stars and production personnel, many of whom are pleased to attend.

Xeroxed and self-published *Dark Shadows* fanzines blossomed throughout the 1980s, two of the most important being *Shadowgram* (designed to keep fans apprised of events related to the show and its cast) and *The World of "Dark Shadows"* (which ran short stories, poetry, drawings, etc., sent in by fans). Other fanzines of the era included *Wyndcliffe [sic] Watch* and *Inside the Old House,* as well as numerous single publications and more local fan club bulletins. Fannish activity burgeoned throughout the early 1990s with the arrival of the remake series in 1991, the video release of the original series on MPI Video, and screenings on the Sci-Fi channel. During those years, *Dark Shadows* fandom was comprised of approximately equal numbers of men and women, and that has not changed much in subsequent decades. Many fans from that era were children or teenagers during the show's initial run, and their nostalgic memories of childhood were important to their ongoing participation in *Dark Shadows* fandom. Today's *Dark Shadows* fans include newer and younger participants who continue to discover the show in one or many of its multiple forms.

Examination of *Dark Shadows* fanzines from the 1990s reveals fans' interests in certain recurring themes derived from the primary text(s): vampirism, time travel, romance, and love as a force capable of transcending time and history. Barnabas Collins figures prominently in many of the stories, drawings, songs, and skits. The majority of the stories that were serious in tone were written by women; conversely, most of the stories with a comedic edge were written by men, although there were certainly exceptions to these generalizations. Several of the most interesting story trends used *Dark Shadows* to address the changing nature of gender roles, especially as they applied to the time-traveling character of Dr. Julia Hoffman. Others bordered on soft-core gothic romance, masking sex and sexuality behind the genre's usual monstrous signifiers. Compared to contemporary fans, many of those writing in the 1990s seemed somewhat reticent to include frank or explicit depictions of sex and sexuality in their work, perhaps fearing reprisals from other fans or the show's producers. For example, the attempt to start a specifically gay and lesbian fanzine devoted to the show never materialized (as far as I can tell), and slashzines based on *Dark Shadows* characters were hard to locate in the mid-1990s; many *Dark Shadows* fans had never heard of slash.

Dark Shadows slash can now be found easily on the web. Slash fictions are fan-produced texts that posit a homosexual relationship between two male leads on a particular television show: in the case of *Star Trek*, K/S slash depicts sex and love between Captain Kirk and Mr. Spock, often complete with graphic drawings and descriptions of sexual acts. Constance Penley, in her groundbreaking research on the subject, reported that these stories were initially produced mostly by and for heterosexual female fans, arguing that they reconfigure heterosexual romance through a homosexual matrix. As she argued, slash relationships are seemingly dependent on the equality of their participants, making use of a homosexual premise to reimagine a heterosexual union between two "truly equal" partners, neatly sidestepping the culturally encoded "inequality" inherent in heterosexual relationships. Interestingly, most of the homosocial male-male pairs that *Dark Shadows* constructs are not based on equality but are instead bounded by rigid power hierarchies: between men and boys (Quentin and Jameson, for example) or between master and servant (Barnabas and Ben, Barnabas and Willie, or Count Petofi and his foppish pretty-boy assistant, Aristede). Perhaps because of that, some of the more common *Dark Shadows* slash fictions found on the web today are primarily "crossover" texts—"mash ups" that combine *Dark Shadows* characters with those from related shows like *Buffy the Vampire Slayer* or *Angel*.

Other slash texts de-repress the homosexuality inherent in some of the original show's story lines. For example, the two-part video *Dark Shadows of the Closet* by TheVampireSara recuts and reimagines the Barnabas/Willie/Jason story line from 1967, making it seem as though Willie is dumping Jason in order to be with his new lover Barnabas. In part 2, several months later in the original story line, Willie is refigured as a spurned lover, jealous of the attentions that Barnabas is now lavishing on Julia and/or Victoria Winters. Similarly, after the popularity of *Brokeback Mountain* (2005), scareolyn mashed up Barnabas and Willie with cowboys Ennis Del Mar and Jack Twist, "recasting" Angelique and Carolyn as their wives desperately trying to understand the nature of their homosexual relationship (*Brokeback Shadows Trailer*).

Given the queer nature of gothic horror, it is not surprising that *Dark Shadows* fandom is tied to gay and lesbian communities in many suggestive ways. As early as 1991, the *Dark Shadows* Fan Club of Southern California was listed in the *Los Angeles Gay and Lesbian Community Yellow Pages* under the classification "Lesbian and Gay Community Resources, Organizations, and Survival Services." The number of gay and lesbian people participating in the annual conventions also seems far greater than recent demographic statistics (3–4 percent of the population) would suggest. At the 1992 Halloween *Dark Shadows* Convention in Los Angeles, literal signifiers of gay and lesbian political power (including red AIDS ribbons, "Lesbian and Gay Men for Clinton" buttons, and "Censorship is UnAmerican" T-shirts) were out in abundance. And although some fans were reluctant to discuss those aspects of the show's appeal in the 1990s— as evidenced by some internecine squabbles among different factions—they have become fairly commonplace topics in recent years, with even the show's stars willing to acknowledge the queerness at Collinwood. At one recent convention, John Karlen discussed the sadomasochistic angle to Willie's relationship with Barnabas, and David Selby said that he always felt "Quentin secretly wanted to be bitten by Barnabas." The rise of the web has allowed for almost microscopically focused fan forums devoted to every type of *Dark Shadows* fan, including the Jimmy_Storm_Club "intended for homosexual fans of James" Storm (the dark and brooding actor who played Gerard Collins), Chickslash (exploring female-female relationships in fantasy shows), and the self-explanatory ShadowsSmut Yahoo! group.

As many gay fans have pointed out, Barnabas Collins had his own "fag hag," a close but nonsexual female friend, in the person of Dr. Julia Hoffman. Her unrequited love for Barnabas can be read as one aspect of the gay experience. As one fan from the 1990s noted, "Gays know what she must be going through every time she looks at Barnabas with those 'I love you' eyes, and he simply ignores her" (quoted in Benshoff, "Secrets," 210). In addition, "Grayson Hall as Dr. Julia Hoffman" is a central anchor of the show's camp appeal. Grayson Hall's over-melodramatized style of performance, coupled with her mannish manner, have led to a plethora of fan-made texts where (gay) male fans impersonate the great lady in assorted skits and videos. Among the most amusing of these are Richard Halpern's *Baby Dark Shadows* videos, many of which feature Halpern as Julia Hoffman (with his niece and nephew playing everyone else at Collinwood).

Another early video text with a male fan playing Julia Hoffman is *A Doctor Remembers,* a clever twenty-minute faux documentary made in 1985 by Tom Soderberg and Owen Robertson. In it, Dr. Julia Hoffman (played by Soderberg) reminisces about her years spent at Collinwood; the tape is full of witty intertextual references as well as Soderberg mimicking Hall's exaggerated mannerisms and style of speech. Julia mentions that she is up for a part in Aaron Spelling's newest television show, *Dark Mansions,* and an alleged photo of her father, Judge Herman Hoffman, reveals gay cast member Louis Edmonds as he was then appearing on another soap opera, *All My Children.* Julia also tells us that Vicky has run off with a millionaire who supposedly murdered his wife, an allusion to actress Alexandra Moltke's connection to the von Bulow trial. Soderberg-as-Hoffman satirizes many of the show's more outlandish credibility gaps in a deadpan style of delivery. Standing in the woods between Collinwood and the Old House, Julia remembers how she used to go from "one house to the other, one house to the other, one house to the other . . . at the end of a busy night I'd go to bed quite dizzy." Julia also discusses her ability to wear so many different hats: "You see, besides being an M.D., blood specialist, biologist, and family historian, I'm also a licensed psychologist." Ultimately, Julia confesses to the camera and comes to "realize and confront the truth, that yes, I had a love-jones" (for Barnabas).

Contemporary videos that focus on Julia Hoffman/Grayson Hall run the gamut from outright mocking to devoted love, again capturing the essence of the show's camp appeal. For example, *DarkShadowsJuliaHysterics2* by Tim and Troy is a short excerpt of an actual episode in which Hoffman/Hall is shown at her laughing-screaming-sobbing excessive best. On the other hand, Chatroomchi's montage of Julia (listed on YouTube as *Dark Shadows—Julia*) features images cut to the Beatles' soft ballad "Julia" and is a true love letter to the character/actress, as is the heartfelt *In Memory of Grayson Hall aka Julia Hoffman*

Grayson Hall as Dr. Julia Hoffman still commands a large gay male fan following: when not sobbing, screaming, or offering sedatives to other hysterical women, she could also be quite professionally elegant.

by SxyBabyBoy01. Other wags have produced videos suggesting that Julia was transgendered. Naboomboo's *Dear Julia (Music Video)* shows nothing but a man in drag overacting as Julia while the lyrics extol the virtues of a transgendered lover:

> She's part girl
> She's part boy
> She's got parts everyone can enjoy.

A few gay fans even use drag to mock other fans: the *Dark Shadows Sutherland Show* appears to be a send up of fanzine editor May Sutherland, with two men impersonating the devoted fan hosting a bargain-basement talk show. A skit by gay fans at one recent convention drew explicit links between *Dark*

Shadows and *Dante's Cove* (2005) and *The Lair* (2007), two soft-core gothic serials that aired on the gay pay-per-view channel Here-TV! What was once a closeted subtext of the gothic television serial is now a prominent aspect of explicitly gay niche marketing.

That said, in the Internet age there are *Dark Shadows* websites designed to appeal to just about any fan, from star-based sites that seek to promote or sell related items, to fictionalized monster sex sites, to sites devoted to ingenues Carolyn Stoddard and Victoria Winters. Still more sites are intertextual, devoted to discussing *Dark Shadows* within the ever-expanding universe of horror and fantasy texts. As of this date, *Dark Shadows* exhibits few signs of disappearing from the pop culture horizon.

Dark Shadows 2008

Just as they had for some thirty-odd years, in July of 2008 thousands of *Dark Shadows* fans gathered for an annual convention held that year at the Marriott Hotel and Convention Center in Burbank, California. The hottest buzz of the year was the news that Johnny Depp had recently purchased the rights to *Dark Shadows* with the intention of adapting it for the big screen. Frequent Depp collaborator (and fellow *Dark Shadows* fan) Tim Burton was rumored to be in talks with Depp about directing the project, and it was announced that a screenplay was being written by another Burton alumnus, John August. Most fans were thrilled that Depp and Burton were attached to the project. Fans knew that Burton has made a career for himself by self-consciously reimagining the tone and/or content of classic horror and fantasy texts (*Batman* [1989], *Edward Scissorhands* [1990], *Sleepy Hollow* [1999], *Charley and the Chocolate Factory* [2005], *Sweeney Todd* [2008]), while the soft-spoken yet intense Johnny Depp was seen as the ideal casting choice for Barnabas. Fans also spent considerable time "dream casting" other roles: Helena Bonham Carter as Dr. Hoffman? Uma Thurman as Angelique? Perhaps Angelina Jolie? Fans were also told that probably the only way they would ever see a restored version of *Night of Dark Shadows* was if the new Depp/Burton film found commercial success, thus making its restoration and DVD rerelease economically feasible.

Also on display at the 2008 convention was the rarely seen first episode of the aborted WB network version of *Dark Shadows* made in 2004. Following that network's usual formula, the show was cast considerably younger than either the original series or its 1991 remake, and its regimen of sex and violence was similarly increased for more modern-day audiences. One of its more contemporary casting choices was Kelly Hu as a very young Asian American Dr. Julia Hoffman (a choice many fans disagreed with); Scottish actor Alec Newman as Barnabas was more warmly received by the fans in attendance. Perhaps the most interesting thing about the pilot was its luridly lit visual design, one more reminiscent of Italian horror films by Mario Bava and/or Dario Argento than the original series. It was apparent, however, that the producers had not found a way to create and maintain a consistent tone for the show, with some scenes played straightforwardly while others seemed deliberately over-the-top. In that respect, trying to re-create *Dark Shadows* as deliberate camp rather than naive camp may have doomed the project from its outset.

Another batch of "new" *Dark Shadows* texts displayed at the convention eschews visual design all together: *Dark Shadows Reborn* is a series of original dramas on audio CD starring original cast members David Selby, Lara Parker, John Karlen, and Kathryn Leigh Scott. Developed by the British firm Big Finish Productions (which produces similar CDs based on other cult texts like *Doctor Who* [BBC, 1963–89, 2005–] and *Stargate: Atlantis* [Sci-Fi, 2004–9]), the audio dramas aim to recapture the feel of the original 1960s show. Judging by the number of blind or seeing-impaired convention attendees in 2008, this audio series has generated an entirely new group of fans. In many ways, *Dark Shadows Reborn* looks back to the show's roots in early radio broadcasts of mystery-terror shows like *Lights Out*

(1934–47) and *Inner Sanctum* (1941–52), as well as the early days of radio soap operas. It also underlines the fact that televisual soap operas—*Dark Shadows* included—are highly dependent on sound and that in many cases they were designed to be heard as much as viewed by "distracted" housewives (Altman, "Television Sound"; Modleski, *Loving*). However, in the case of *Dark Shadows*—as we have seen—both aural and visual elements contribute to a sense of televisual excess that elicits highly engaged—not distracted—viewing practices (Caldwell, *Televisuality*).

Jonathan Frid, who has only rarely appeared at fan conventions over the years, did appear in 2008, emerging from a coffin with the aid of John "Willie Loomis" Karlen, in effect re-creating Barnabas's first appearance on the show. (Some wags noted that

Lara Parker as the witch Angelique, here looking rather demur and worried (for a change); more recently Lara Parker has also written *Dark Shadows* novels and contributed to original *Dark Shadows* audio dramas.

the elder Frid needed considerable help getting out of the coffin.) Frid declined to appear with the rest of the cast during a group question and answer session; instead he presented his own clip show titled "The Growth of Barnabas." Frid also declined to sign autographs with the rest of the stars, answer any questions related to his personal life, or even answer a female fan's question regarding Barnabas's ongoing sexual appeal. David Selby, on the other hand, was much more open about life and politics, entering the packed hall while tossing confetti and shouting, "Quentin Collins for President!" In a long and rambling speech, Selby recounted the story of his new book *Lincoln's Better Angel* and discussed what it was like appearing on *Dark Shadows* while the war in Vietnam raged and civil rights leaders were assassinated. As the only cast member to discuss politics that day, Selby drew comparisons between Vietnam and the war in Iraq and took the opportunity to stump for Barack Obama.

It remains to be seen what the future holds for the *Dark Shadows* franchise. What would the show's many crystal balls and tarot cards suggest about its future incarnations? Did they predict its ongoing influence back in the late 1960s? Stay tuned. If the feature film is produced and becomes a hit, it would certainly pump new life into the franchise, even though as an almost fifty-year-old "living corpse" *Dark Shadows* remains pretty lively via its DVD afterlife, multiple appeals, robust fandoms, and occasional new "professional" incarnations like the *Dark Shadows Reborn* audio CDs. There are precious few television shows, let alone daytime soap operas, that have been as unique, long lasting, and influential as *Dark Shadows* has been. It truly is a milestone in the history of American television and media culture.

Allen, Robert C. "Soap Opera." *Museum of Broadcast Communications.*
www.museum.tv/archives/etv/S/htmlS/soapopera/soapopera.htm
(accessed February 4, 2009).

———. *Speaking of Soap Operas.* Chapel Hill: University of North Caro-
lina Press, 1985.

———, ed. *To Be Continued: Soap Operas around the World.* London: Routledge, 1995.

Altman, Rick. "Television Sound." In *Television: The Critical View,* 4th ed.,
edited by Horace Newcomb, 566–84. New York: Oxford University
Press, 1987.

Amory, Cleveland. Review of *Dark Shadows* (ABC). *TV Guide,* February 1,
1969, 6.

Ang, Ien. *Watching "Dallas."* London: Methuen, 1985.

Barthel, Joan. "Out in Detergent Land: A Hard Day's Fright." *New York
Times,* July 30, 1967.

Benshoff, Harry M. "Resurrection of the Vampire: *Dark Shadows* and Fan
Culture." *Spectator,* Spring 1993, 50–61.

———. "Secrets, Closets, and Corridors through Time: Negotiating Sexuality and Gender in *Dark Shadows* Fan Culture." In *Theorizing Fandom: Fans, Subcultures, and Identity,* edited by Cheryl Harris and Ali-
son Alexander, 199–218. Creskill, NJ: Hampton Press, 1998.

Brockman, Michael. "Interview." Collection 2, Disc 4. *Dark Shadows: The
Beginning,* DVD. Orland Park, IL: MPI Home Video, 2002.

Brown, Mary Ellen. *Soap Opera and Women's Talk.* London: Sage, 1994.

————, ed. *Television and Women's Culture*. London: Sage, 1990.

Caldwell, John Thornton. *Televisuality: Style, Crisis, and Authority in American Television*. New Brunswick, NJ: Rutgers University Press, 1995.

Efron, Edith. "No Tears for Miss Bennett." *TV Guide*, August 26, 1967, 12–14.

Feehan, Margaret. Letter to the Editor. *TV Guide,* May 1, 1971, A2.

Feuer, Jane. "Melodrama, Serial Form and Television Today." *Screen* 25, no. 1 (1984): 4–16.

Fox, George. "Can a 172-Year-Old Vampire Find Love and Happiness in a Typical New England Town?" *Saturday Evening Post*, November 30, 1968, 40–41, 80–81.

Geraghty, Christine. *Women and Soap Opera*. Cambridge: Polity Press, 1991.

"The Ghoul Show." *Newsweek,* August 21, 1967, 60.

"Giddy Gothic." *TV Guide,* December 3, 1966, 12–13.

Gillespie, Marie. *Television, Ethnicity and Cultural Change*. London: Routledge, 1995.

Grainge, Paul. *Brand Hollywood: Selling Entertainment in a Global Media Age*. London: Routledge, 2008.

Greenberg, Harvey Roy. "*King Kong*: The Beast in the Boudoir." In *The Dread of Difference*, edited by Barry K. Grant, 338–51. Austin: University of Texas Press, 1996.

Guerrero, Ed. *Framing Blackness: The African American Image in Film*. Philadelphia: Temple University Press, 1993.

Haggerty, George E. *Queer Gothic*. Urbana: University of Illinois Press, 2006.

Hall, Stuart, Dorothy Hobson, Andrew Lowe, and Paul Willis, eds. *Culture Media Language*. London: Unwin Hyman, 1980.

Hamrick, Craig. *Barnabas and Company: The Cast of the TV Classic "Dark Shadows."* New York: iUniverse Star, 2003.

————. *Big Lou: The Life and Career of Actor Louis Edmonds*. New York: iUniverse Star, 2003.

Higgins, Robert. "More Perils Than Pauline: Kathryn Leigh Scott is the Super Victim of Daytime TV." *TV Guide*, May 31, 1969, 16–17.

Hills, Matt. "Defining Cult TV: Texts, Intertexts and Fan Audiences." In *The Television Studies Reader*, edited by Robert C. Allen and Annette Hill, 509–23. London: Routledge, 2004.

Hobson, Dorothy. *Soap Opera*. Cambridge: Polity Press, 2003.

Jenkins, Henry. *Convergence Culture: Where Old and New Media Collide*.

New York: New York University Press, 2006.

———. *Textual Poachers: Television Fans and Participatory Culture*. New York: Routledge, 1992.

Joyrich, Lynne. "All That Television Allows: TV Melodrama, Postmodernism, and Consumer Culture." *Camera Obscura* 16 (January 1988): 129–53.

Katz, E., and T. Liebes. "Mutual Aid in the Decoding of *Dallas*: Preliminary Notes from a Cross-Cultural Study." *Media, Culture and Society* 5, no. 2 (1983): 179–97.

Lamberson, Greg. "Remembering *Dark Shadows* with *Path of Fate* Author Stephen Mark Rainey." *Fear Zone*. www.fearzone.com/blog/dark-rainey (accessed May 27, 2009).

Levine, Elana. "Toward a Paradigm for Media Production Research: Behind the Scenes at *General Hospital*." In *Television: The Critical View*, 7th ed., edited by Horace Newcomb, 133–49. New York: Oxford University Press, 2007.

MacAndrew, Elizabeth. *The Gothic Tradition in Fiction*. New York: Columbia University Press, 1970.

Mathijs, Ernest, and Xavier Mendik. *The Cult Film Reader*. England: McGraw Hill/Open University Press, 2008.

Meyer, Moe, ed. *The Politics and Poetics of Camp*. New York: Routledge, 1994.

Miller, D. A. *The Novel and the Police*. Berkeley: University of California Press, 1988.

Miller, Daniel. "*The Young and the Restless* in Trinidad: A Case of the Local and the Global in Mass Communication." In *Consuming Technologies: Media and Information in Domestic Spaces*, edited by R. Silverstone and E. Hirsch, 163–82. London: Routledge, 1992.

Mittell, Jason. "Narrative Complexity in Contemporary American Television." *Velvet Light Trap* 58 (Fall 2006): 29–40.

Modleski, Tania. *Loving with a Vengeance*. Hamden, CT: Archon Books, 1982.

Newman, Michael Z. "From Beats to Arcs: Toward a Poetics of Television Narrative." *Velvet Light Trap* 58 (Fall 2006): 16–28.

Penley, Constance. "Brownian Motion: Women, Tactics, and Technology." In *Technoculture*, edited by Constance Penley and Andrew Ross, 135–62. Minneapolis: University of Minnesota Press, 1991.

Pierson, Jim. *"Dark Shadows" Resurrected*. Universal City, CA: Pomegranate Press, 1992.

Santo, Avi. "*Batman* versus *The Green Hornet*: The Merchandisable TV Text and the Paradox of Licensing in the Classical Network Era." *Cinema Journal* 49, no. 2 (2010): 63–85.

Sconce, Jeffrey. "What If? Charting Television's New Textual Boundaries." In *Television After TV: Essays on a Medium in Transition*, edited by Lynn Spigel and Jan Olsson, 93–112. Durham: Duke University Press, 2004.

Scott, Kathryn Leigh. *My Scrapbook Memories of "Dark Shadows."* Los Angeles: Pomegranate Press, 1986.

———, ed. *The "Dark Shadows" Companion.* Universal City, CA: Pomegranate Press, 1990.

———, and Jim Pierson, eds. *"Dark Shadows" Almanac: Millennium Edition.* Beverly Hills, CA: Pomegranate Press, 2000.

Seiter, Ellen, H. Borchers, G. Kreutzner, and E. Warth, eds. *Remote Control: Television Audiences and Cultural Power.* London: Routledge, 1989.

"Ship of Ghouls." *Time*, August 20, 1968.

Skal, David J. *The Monster Show: A Cultural History of Horror.* Rev. ed. New York: Faber and Faber, 2001.

Sontag, Susan. "Notes on Camp." In *A Susan Sontag Reader*, by Susan Sontag, 105–20. New York: Vintage Books, 1983.

Spigel, Lynn. "From Domestic Space to Outer Space." In *Close Encounters: Film, Feminism, and Science Fiction*, edited by Constance Penley et al., 5–35. Minneapolis: University of Minnesota Press, 1991.

Thomas, Kevin. "Familiar Look to 'Shadows' Sequel." Review of *Night of Dark Shadows. Los Angeles Times*, n.d.

Thompson, Jeff. *The Television Horrors of Dan Curtis.* Jefferson, NC: McFarland, 2009.

Thorburn, David. "Television Melodrama." In *Television: The Critical View*, 4th ed., edited by Horace Newcomb, 628–44. New York: Oxford University Press, 1987.

Tulloch, John, and Henry Jenkins. *Science Fiction Audiences: Watching "Doctor Who" and "Star Trek."* London: Routledge, 1995.

"Turned-On Vampire." *Newsweek*, April 20, 1970, 102–3.

Waters, Harry F. "New Sins in Soapland." *Newsweek*, December 9, 1968, 100–104.

Wheatley, Helen. *Gothic Television.* Manchester: Manchester University Press, 2006.

Williams, Linda. "Film Bodies: Gender, Genre, and Excess." *Film Quarterly* 44, no. 4 (1991): 2–13.

Wood, Robin. *Hollywood: From Vietnam to Reagan*. New York: Columbia University Press, 1986.

Worland, Rick. "*Dark Shadows*, 1970: The Leviathan Plotline and the Return of the Repressed." Unpublished manuscript.

Zanger, Jules. "From Metaphor to Metonymy." In *Blood Read: The Vampire in Contemporary Culture*, edited by Joan Gordon and Veronica Hollinger, 17–26. Philadelphia: University of Pennsylvania Press, 1997.

129